how to

Use the Internet in ELT

Dede Teeler
with Peta Gray

Longman

series editor:
Jeremy Harmer

Pearson Education Limited
Edinburgh Gate
Harlow
Essex CM20 2JE
England
and Associated Companies throughout the World

www.longman-elt.com

© Pearson Education Limited 2000

First published 2000
Second impression 2000

Printed in Malaysia, PJB

Produced for the publishers by Bluestone Press, Charlbury, Oxfordshire, UK
Text design by Keith Rigley at White Horse Graphics

ISBN 0582 339316

For Mark
because there is nothing permanent but change

Contents

Acknowledgements

We are indebted to the following for permission to reproduce copyright material:
Cambridge University Press for an adapted extract and diagram from *Language in Use Pre-Intermediate Classroom Book* by Adrian Doff and Christopher Jones, CUP (1991); the author, Carolyn Fidelman of Agora Language Market Place for an adapted extract and diagram from *Agora Newsletter* January 1997 (special report); Pearson Education for an adapted extract from *Towards Task-based Language Learning*, edited by Candlin and Murphy, Prentice Hall (1987).

Photograph page 5: Gareth Boden
Picture researcher: Rebecca Watson

We are grateful to the following for permission to use screens from their web sites:

Page 14: *Netscape Communicator* screenshots © 1999 Netscape Communications Corporation. Used with Permission

Page 18: Dave Sperling, *Dave's ESL cafe*: http://www.eslcafe.com

Page 21: University of Manchester, Continuing Education, copyright The University of Manchester

Page 23: IATEFL *Electronic JobShop*

Page 27: *Tile.Net*, Lyris Technologies

Page 30: *Netscape Communicator* screenshots © 1999 Netscape Communications Corporation. Used with Permission

Page 32: International House Barcelona, chat channel

Page 33: *Worlds Ultimate 3D chat* by worlds.com

Page 34: schMOOze University founded by Julie Falsetti and Eric Schweitzer. Text from Neteach-L archives: http://spot.colorado.edu/~youngerg/log19-a.html

Page 49: *Autonomy Agentware*, copyright Autonomy Corporation PLC

Page 66: *Plumb Design's Visual Thesaurus* was developed by Plumb Design using its proprietary Thinkmap software. More information is available about Thinkmap at: http://www.thinkmap.com

Page 67: Forgotten Houses Ltd. Unusual holiday homes in Cornwall

Page 69: *Teen Advice Online*™, copyright Teen Advice Online

Page 73: MysteryNet's *TheCase.com* features online solvable mysteries © Newfront Productions Inc.

Page 74: reproduced with permission © 1998 Exploratorium, http://www.exploratorium.com

Page 76: *Asiaquest*, copyright *Classroom Connect*, http://www.classroom.com

Page 78: *BBC Radio 5 Live*, copyright the BBC; *Realplayer*™ copyright © 1995–1999 RealNetworks, Inc. All rights reserved. *RealNetworks*, *RealAudio*, *RealVideo*, and *RealPlayer* are trademarks or registered trademarks of RealNetworks, Inc.

Disclaimer:
We have made efforts to trace all owners of copyright material but in a few cases listed below in page order this has not proved possible and we therefore take this opportunity to apologise to any copyright holders whose rights we may have unwittingly infringed.

Pages 2, 3, 8, 10, 18, 20, 24, 26, 27, 29, 38, 40, 43–46, 47, 48, 51, 72.

Author's Acknowledgements

To the many friends and colleagues that have aided and abetted over the year it took to finally write this book, a heartfelt thanks. Your warm comments and sincere criticisms have been cherished.

I am especially indebted to Peta Gray, who spent many a late night discussing the text and experimenting on the Internet so that she could sketch out the task files you see in this final version. My apologies to her family, who got to see so little of her.

Thanks once again to Jane Stanley for her original idea about using the Teen Advice web site, adapted for the activity in Chapter 5. I would also like to express my thanks to Jane and Dave Willis for lending me a cheery space to write, and for making me take breaks at just the right moments.

The enthusiastic feedback I received from colleagues and virtual colleagues at various workshops, training sessions and conferences has likewise been invaluable to me. A very special thanks to Ruth Vilmi, Dennis Oliver, Paul Brett, Christine Melowi, Mike McCay, Anne McCabe, Anne Zanatta, Mark Hinchliff, Evelyn Byrne, Bella Campillo, Mario Rinvolucri, Trish Delamere, Eamon Roche, Andy Hopkins and Claire Burns, as well as to the committee members of the IATEFL Computer Special Interest Group, whose early morning debates actually spurred me into putting these words on paper.

Of course, I could not have written this book without the enthusiastic support and extraordinary patience of the series editor Jeremy Harmer, whose observations were always clear and perceptive. And my infinite gratitude to the person whose dedication and precision has made the text into what you see here, Brigit Viney. Thank you.

Finally, I would like to express my profound appreciation to that rare and remarkable computer expert who taught me nearly everything I know about these tools, often as not against my will. Thanks to my mother, Melissa E. Gray, without whom this book would not have been written.

Introduction

Who is this book for?

How to Use the Internet in ELT is a book for teachers of English who have little or no experience of the **Internet** and are intrigued to discover how to master it for the benefit of themselves and their students. Those more experienced with the Internet may also find ideas and resources described in the book that can extend their knowledge and skills.

What is it about?

- The first chapter gives a general guide to the character and history of the international communications system known as the Internet. It then offers an overview of the main facilities available on the Internet and, in particular, **e-mail**, the electronic postal system, and the **World Wide Web**.
- Chapter 2 discusses how the Internet offers a virtual teachers' room packed with resources and information available to teachers for their own professional development.
- Chapter 3 takes the reader on a step-by-step tour through the facilities available on the Internet for finding materials that can then be used directly with students, or adapted to suit their particular needs. It also addresses the issue of copyright protection of materials contained on the Internet.
- Chapter 4 describes an Internet classroom and looks at ways of setting one up and then managing it, and discusses the differences between managing an Internet classroom and a conventional one.
- Chapter 5 looks at a wide variety of activities (each focusing on language study, listening, speaking, reading or writing) that can be used in the Internet classroom, and discusses how to design and set up the activities.
- Chapter 6 suggests that we can even see the Internet as a source of language work in place of a coursebook, and outlines ways of developing and designing an Internet-based language course.
- The Task File contains a number of activities related to the content of each chapter to give the reader the opportunity to review their understanding of the chapter and reflect on what they have read.
- The Glossary (pages 102–105) lists and explains the technical terms used in the book. Terms that appear in the Glossary are printed in bold within the book.
- At the end of the book are five appendices. The first is about e-mail programs. The second gives examples of **newsgroups**, and the third gives examples of **mailing lists** all available via the Internet. The fourth appendix gives a list of **web sites** of interest to language teachers, and the final appendix offers suggestions for further reading.

How to Use the Internet in ELT can be read from cover to cover or readers can use it as reference source for information or ideas on particular issues and needs related to the teacher's use of the Internet.

What is the Internet?

It would appear that we have reached the limits of what it is possible to achieve with computer technology, although I should be careful with such statements, as they tend to sound pretty silly in 5 years.
John von Neumann, circa 1949

- **What is the Internet?**
- **A bit of history**
- **Applications and their uses**
- **Are teachers using the Internet?**
- **How to use basic e-mail**
- **What is Netiquette?**
- **What is a web browser?**
- **How to use a web browser**
- **Navigating the Web**

What is the Internet?

We live in the age of the computer, and there are growing demands on almost everyone, including teachers, to become technologically literate. You may already use computer programs to create materials for students, but you may feel confused, or intimidated, by the publicity about the Internet and the jargon people use to talk about it. The **Internet** – alias the **Net** – is also known as cyberspace, the information superhighway, the online community, the electronic library and the digital revolution: all a series of creative metaphors trying to define it. It has been hyped as the most significant development in communication tools since the invention of the printing press and then condemned as the end of civilisation as we know it. So, what is it?

Basically, the Internet is a network of people and information, linked together by telephone lines which are connected to computers. In fact, more than 100,000 independent networks – public and private – are currently connected to form this vast global communications system. This is the 'road' of the information superhighway.

There are many ways to transport information on this highway, through the various **application** programs such as **e-mail** and the **World Wide Web**. All of these applications are based on a client/server relationship, in which your computer is the client, and a remote computer is the server. Your computer asks for files, and formats the information it receives. The information is actually stored on a remote computer, and is sent to you over the telephone line at your request, usually at the click of a mouse.

All you need to join this system is a computer, a normal telephone line, a **modem** and an account with an Internet Service Provider (**ISP**).

- **Computer**: almost any computer can be used to connect to the Internet. However, this is your personal lane on the information superhighway. The slower your computer is, the slower the traffic in your lane will be when sending and receiving information. To take advantage of the **multimedia** components that are available – the video, audio and interactive elements of the Net – it is almost mandatory to have a powerful PC or Apple home computer because multimedia files are much larger than pure text files.

- **Telephone line**: your computer will use your normal telephone line to transport data while you are connected. There is no need to have a second line installed, though there are some obvious disadvantages to having only one line. The size of your telephone line can also seriously affect the quality and speed of your **access**. A couple of alternatives to the traditional telephone connection are described in Chapter 4 in the section on access speeds (see page 58).

- **Modem**: this is a small piece of equipment that translates the **digital** language your computer speaks into the **analogue** language used by the telephone, thereby enabling you to send and receive data. The name is a shortened form of modulate–demodulate (translation to analogue-translation to digital). Most new computers are sold with a modem already installed. If yours was not, you will need to do a bit of research into the latest models, to get the best speed and compatibility.

- **Internet Service Provider**: an **ISP** is a company that acts as a toll gate between you and the Internet. You pay them an annual fee for unlimited use of the Net, or monthly charges according to the amount of time you are actually connected. These companies do not control the content of the Internet, nor how any of it functions, but they offer you access to the Internet.

  Most countries have a wide range of ISPs on offer, so it is best to shop around before you choose one. You should look for an ISP with a local telephone number or you will be paying long-distance telephone call rates. In addition, you will need a supportive company to start with, one that gives you all the software, help setting it up, at least one e-mail account and perhaps even free space to have your own site on the World Wide Web.

And that's really all you need to become a part of the online community.

A bit of history
So how did this modern wonder come into existence? In a nutshell, the first version of the Internet was started during the 1960s in the United States as ARPAnet, a defence department network. One computer was linked to another to share information. Gradually, more computers were added to the network, and people began to send simple messages over the network to distant colleagues. This, at that time, incredible communications platform

was adopted by the academic community and, with vast improvements added by European computer wizards, became the friendly tool we refer to as the Internet today.

As a form of international communication, the Internet has been in constant expansion since 1973, when the ARPAnet was first connected to the United Kingdom and Norway. Much of northern Europe was connected to the Net in the early 1980s. Japan and Canada soon followed suit. A special link was established between Germany and China at about the same time. And then in the late 1980s the real growth began as Australia, Iceland, Israel, Italy, Mexico, New Zealand and Puerto Rico joined the Net.

The early 1990s saw many countries in South America and Asia, as well as Eastern Europe, gain access to the Net. The first countries connected from the African continent were Tunisia and South Africa, but others soon followed. By 1992, even Antarctica was officially online. Currently every nation has some type of connection to the Internet, though access may be highly restricted and extremely expensive.

Because of its origin in the United States, most of the communication via the Internet takes place in English, in spite of, or perhaps due to, the multilingual nature of its user base. Researchers suggest that this will change as the Internet becomes more popular, but for the moment English is the common language. This is what makes it such a perfect tool for English language teaching.

Applications and their uses

Like many of the modern conveniences we now take for granted, the Net had primitive beginnings. (The Model T, the camera obscura and the wireless telegraph were all innovations that initially required expert handling. Despite this, almost all of us can now drive a car, take a photograph or use the phone.) Most of the current text-only Internet tools are leftovers from a bygone era of more primitive computer technology. As the Net incorporates more and more multimedia features some of these text-only **applications** become obsolete, some are superseded by more user-friendly programs, and others are adapted. The key text-based applications that remain are:

- **E-mail**: This is the electronic postal service.

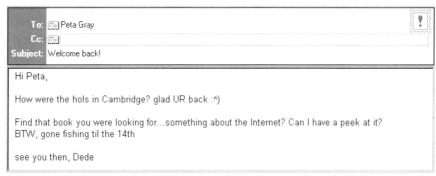

An example of an e-mail message

Its traditional counterpart is known as snail mail, so at first glance the most obvious benefit of using e-mail is speed. It is so fast that you can send written messages back and forth to people several times a day. It is a cost-effective, reliable form of communication that lets you send notes to other Internet users around the globe from the comfort of your own computer. You can also attach enormous documents to that same note so you do not need to send these through the post either. Although they are basically a text-based medium, e-mail programs now make it possible to attach large files, graphics, video or sounds to notes. Some e-mail programs even feature voice-mail so you can listen to your messages. We will take a closer look at how to use basic e-mail later in this chapter (see page 6).

- **Mailing lists**: These are an automated exchange of e-mail messages about a chosen topic, each one being a kind of supervised discussion group. They are often called discussion lists or listservs. We consider **mailing lists** in detail, and explain how to join lists related to teacher development, in Chapter 2 (see page 23).

- **Newsgroups**: The system of **newsgroups** is a worldwide network of open discussion groups on thousands of subjects. They are 'open' in that they are not usually supervised or **moderated** and can be read by anyone that is interested. They are interesting spaces for debate, and there are several dedicated to educational themes. You will find more information on newsgroups in Chapter 2 (see page 28) and in Appendix B (see page 108).

- **Chat**: This kind of program is a popular way to communicate in **real time**, that is, instantaneously. Whatever you type into a **chat** program is immediately visible to the other participants on their computers. You can chat to strangers from around the world who share your hobbies or interests, or even arrange to meet family or friends for a **virtual** reunion. For a further description of chat see Chapter 2 (page 31).

- **MOO**: This is a meeting place on the Net, one of several kinds of multi-user environments that have evolved from adventure games and role-playing simulations. **MOO**s are also used for serious educational purposes; some have special areas with interaction at a slower pace set up for EFL students from around the world. Take a look at the end of Chapter 2 (page 33) for a glimpse into these worlds.

Multimedia uses of the Internet require up-to-date computers and several extra bits of hardware and software. Not everyone has access to these applications, but they have been the real force behind the growth of the Internet over the past several years. They are:

- **Videoconferencing**: This is communicating via a live video link over the Internet. Conferencing and **telephony** applications usually cost no more to use than a local phone call, whether you are speaking to someone across town or on the other side of the world. However, they require a very fast, stable connection to the Net, special software; and of course, a video camera, microphone and speakers. Teachers have been making active use of this technology for several years now, especially in distance education and cross-curricular project work.

Videoconferencing in action

- **The World Wide Web** (**WWW** or Web for short): This is a multimedia resource and communications tool based on **hypertext**, a system of clickable links. When you click on a highlighted word or picture you are magically transported to that location – perhaps the next page in the document or another document altogether. Links are also used to view large pictures and to download video or audio files to your computer. This user-friendly application is the real driving force behind the Internet boom of the 1990s. In fact, it is so popular that you may hear people use the terms Web and Internet interchangeably. This is not so inaccurate as it may seem at first glance, since access to most of the older forms of the Internet is now built into the software for viewing the Web, called a web **browser**. You can read your e-mail, view newsgroup messages, do **videoconferencing** – and gain entry to many other useful programs we have not mentioned here – directly through your web browser. The last section of this chapter (see page 10) is dedicated to the basic operation of this far-reaching application. Appendix D on page 110 lists **web sites** from which you can download software. It also lists sites which help you learn how to use the Internet.

Are teachers using the Internet?

No one really knows how many people are using the Internet. The figures published in the media are quite often just a mixture of informed guesswork and surveys. So how can we know whether teachers are using this technology? And if so, how is it being used by language teachers?

According to teachers' comments – at conferences, in papers and on the Internet mailing lists dedicated to ELT – they seem to use it for just about everything: development, updating language skills, finding materials, learning about computer applications, keeping in touch with friends and colleagues, teaching, working on class projects and activities, and just having fun.

Here are some adapted extracts from a study done by the Agora Language Marketplace. Since 1994, this organisation has been surveying language professionals – teachers, translators and interpreters – about their use of the Internet, and the findings show how teachers' use is increasing in parallel with the tremendous general growth in use of the Web.

The Third Annual Internet Use Survey of Language Professionals
By Carolyn G. Fidelman, *Agora Newsletter*, January 1997 special report

A typical respondent to this survey was female, began using the Internet sometime in mid-1994 ... spends one hour a day reading e-mail, belongs to three discussion lists ... avoids USENET newsgroups, is trying to find some way to integrate this new medium into his or her teaching ... and browses the Web perhaps five hours per week.

If 1994–95 was the year of 'getting on' the Internet, then 1996 was the year of 'getting into' the Net. The results ... indicated a qualitative improvement in the use of this valuable tool for information retrieval, teaching and idea exchange. We have gone from only 26% of those polled having even tried the Web in 1994 to 97% of those polled being regular users this year. Of the 149 web users, over half had employed it in a variety of instructional uses, in the relative percentages shown below:

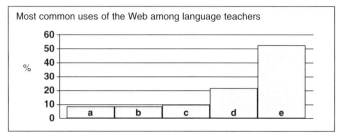

Most common uses of the Web among language teachers

a. **sources of information**: class syllabuses, teachers' links, cultural information, students' home pages
b. **homework**: exercises, printouts for students, other activities
c. **teaching students how to use the Web**
d. **teacher training**
e. **in-class activities**: listening, reading, exploring, information searches, research

---

Several trends seem to be emerging. Computers are becoming increasingly available in schools around the globe. Governments, teachers and parents are advocating the networking of these computers, and making long-range plans for their use at all levels of education. New demands are then being made on teachers to use the technology creatively, leading to a steep rise in the membership of relevant mailing lists and the number of available Internet training courses for teachers. Still, there are many parts of the technology that are not yet being exploited to their full potential, namely the audio and video components, and there is a real lack of substantial research into the pedagogical implications of the technology. However, teachers are showing some clear preferences towards two applications: e-mail and the Web.

How to use basic e-mail

When Queen Elizabeth II sent her first e-mail message in 1976, she did it from an enormous supercomputer with a team of experts to help her. Two decades later the technology has improved so much that we can use it from the privacy of our homes. The interface, the bit of the program you interact with, is so friendly that even small children can send e-mail by themselves. There are two common ways to get e-mail:

- If you travel frequently, or want to read your e-mail in several different locations, you might want to register with one of the hundreds of companies that provide e-mail access through the Web. There is no charge for this service, since advertisers cover most of the operating costs, but there are two definite drawbacks to using Web-based e-mail. Firstly, the services are so popular that access to your mail can be very slow, and secondly, because you must usually be **online** to use the service, you will be paying telephone and ISP charges for the entire time it takes you to read and reply to your messages.

- The customary way of using e-mail is by getting the service from your Internet Service Provider. Most ISPs offer you several e-mail accounts and the software to access them as part of their connections package. This is called **POP** mail. The only time you need to be online is to retrieve or send new messages. You can read and write the replies while you are disconnected from the Internet, saving lots of time and expense.

An e-mail address usually looks something like this:

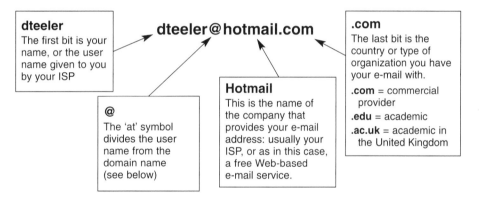

So if I were telling you my address I would say 'My address is d teeler at hotmail dot com.'

E-mail addresses can be much longer of course. But reading them from left to right you will notice that they move from the specific to the general: individual_account@department.organization_name.organization_type.country

The dots are used to separate the **domain name** (the text after the @ sign) into these sections. Careful typing is needed to ensure you make no mistakes, such as leaving extra spaces, transposing letters or changing the case. Dteeler and dTEELER may be different people altogether.

Once you have the address of someone to write to you are pretty well set, and you write a message just as you would type any letter. E-mail then breaks the message down into bite-size packets of information before shipping them around the world at incredible speed to be reunited in the mailbox at the recipient's end. But let's take a closer look at how to begin.

The format of an e-mail message is similar to that of a memo or a fax. Messages are usually short and to the point, and the language is chatty and informal without being discourteous. One way to familiarise yourself with the writing style is to hang around a mailing list for a while and read other people's messages. (See page 23 in Chapter 2 for details of mailing lists.)

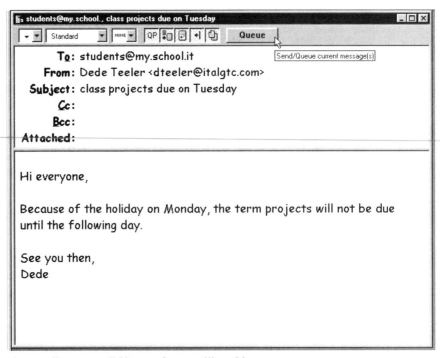

An e-mail message; clicking on Queue will send it

It is always considerate to fill in the subject line with a concise description of the contents of the message, since that may be the only information the recipient has about your message as they sort through their e-mail.

When you have written your message, click on the Send or Queue button to send it to your out-box, a special file for mail waiting to be sent. When you have finished composing several messages, you can connect and send them all at once.

Receiving mail is just as simple. Click on Check Mail from within the File menu. After the program retrieves new messages to your in-box, you can read them at your leisure. To open a message just double-click on it.

After a while you may want to organise the messages you receive into folders called mailboxes. To begin with, an e-mail program usually provides you with an

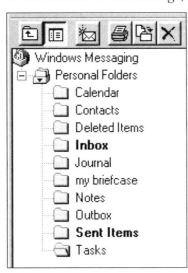

An example of mailbox folders

in-box, for mail you have received; a Sent Items box, for mail you have sent; and a Trash (or Deleted Items) folder, for messages you do not want to keep. You can create as many specific mailboxes as you like, and folders within mailboxes, moving incoming messages to these folders once you have read them.

A favourite e-mail program among language teachers is Eudora Light. It costs nothing, is very simple to use and has excellent help files to get you started, which must be why it is so popular. For instructions on how to personalise this particular e-mail program, see Appendix A (page 106).

What is Netiquette? There are some generally recognised conventions for sending electronic communications, which are collectively known as Netiquette. These standards are basically just common sense mixed with a bit of courtesy, and have developed over the years so that no one forgets that there is a human being at the other end of the telephone line. Here is a rough outline of accepted protocol:

1 **DON'T CAPITALISE EVERYTHING**: It looks as if you are shouting, and it is difficult to read. Save this technique for stressing important points.

2 **Spelling and grammar**: Before you send a message, read through it again and run it through a spellchecker. But remember that e-mail is a high-speed, multicultural form of communication, so be tolerant of other people's errors. People are generally more concerned with getting their message across than worrying about the details.

3 **Length**: Try to imagine yourself as the recipient of the message. How could you make it more concise? Avoid quoting long texts from other people just to say that you agree with them. Shorten your **signature file** to no more than four lines. Everyone is busy, and some people have to pay for e-mail by the line, or by the size of the file.

4 **Multiple recipients**: Being able to send the same message to more than one recipient is a very useful tool, but it can be considered abusive if used too much. Avoid **cross-posting** – sending duplicate messages to various mailing lists and newsgroups – as this can be very annoying for members of those groups. Don't send mass mailings of unsolicited material. This is called **spamming**, and it is condemned by the entire Internet community.

5. **Criticism**: Be careful what you read into other people's messages, because in the absence of paralinguistic information it is easy to misinterpret what others are saying. This is why **smileys**, or emoticons, were invented – as simple ways to express intention. There are many different styles of smiley (you have to tilt your head to the left to understand them!):

:-) simply happy

8° surprised, worried or concerned

=-(sad or cross

Avoid meting out sharp criticism, which is called **flaming**. A simple dry comment could escalate quite rapidly into an all-out war just because the person at the receiving end cannot read your body language or does not share your cultural references.

Since no one entity owns or polices the Net, it is not mandatory to follow any particular rules. However, this advice might help make your experience of the Internet more pleasant. And if you are planning on using the Internet with students, it might be a good idea to run through these notes with them before they go online for the first time.

What is a web browser?

The second application that teachers commonly use is the World Wide Web, a revolutionary idea based on a simple computer coding called **HTML**, hypertext markup language. This language makes it possible to integrate text with photos and multimedia – and connect it all to similar documents with clickable words called **hyperlinks** or **links**. A very simple **web page** looks like this to your computer:

```
<HTML>
<HEAD>
<TITLE>My web page</TITLE>
</HEAD>
<BODY>This is what a basic <a href="page2.html">web page</a>looks like.
</BODY>
</HTML>
```

Hypertext markup language

The bits between <> are called tags, and they tell the software what the web page is supposed to do: link to another page within the **web site**, have a yellow background, show pictures of friends, play a song. In order to read pages written in this code you need a web browser. A web **browser** reads these HTML tags, and presents you with a formatted document you can read. The coding in the box above then appears like this:

A simple web page

There are many web browsers, but the two most popular are Netscape *Navigator* and Microsoft *Internet Explorer*. They are both **freeware**, meaning that they are software programs distributed free of charge. You should receive at least one of these programs bundled into the connection package from your ISP. If not, you will find browsers are often included on the CD-ROMs accompanying computer magazines and books.

Once you have a web browser on your computer, it is easy to **download** a newer version of it from the Internet. This will be handy later, when you run across multimedia files that require a specific browser or helper application.

We take a closer look at multimedia files in Chapter 5, in the section relating to listening activities (see page 77), but for the moment, let's focus on the standard functions of a web browser.

How to use a web browser

When you first open your browser it will often connect to the Internet automatically, taking you right onto the Web. The web page that opens each time you connect is the browser's **home page**, the index page of your program's web site, so that you can get instant help and bulletins about updates to the software you are using.

You will notice that the browser creates a kind of frame around the web page you are viewing. The top part of the frame, which has drop-down menus and a toolbar, looks a bit like a word-processing program.

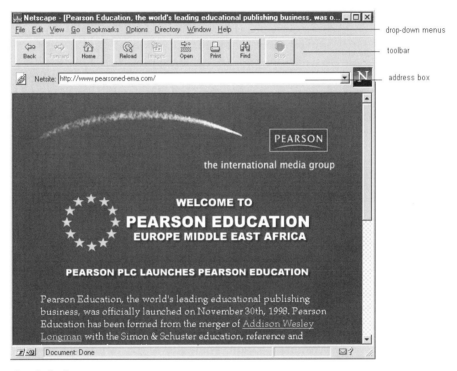

A web site home page

Here you can also find the address box, where the address of the web site appears when you open the browser. To change the address – and visit another web site – you double-click on the text in the box to highlight it, and then just type the new address on top. The moment you start typing the old text disappears. Hit the Enter key and your browser connects to the Internet to find that web site. Once it retrieves it, or downloads it, the new web page will appear in the frame.

The address, or **URL** (uniform resource locator), can be broken down into sections, like the e-mail address we looked at earlier. Here is the address for the home page at the Pearson Education web site:

http
hypertext transfer protocol
This means that you are looking for a Web
document with links and multimedia files

pearsoned-ema.com
is the domain name: the **server**, plus the type
of organization (in this case commercial)

http://www.pearsoned-ema.com

://
This symbol just divides the type
of document or protocol from
the domain name on the right

www
The World Wide Web

Names designed for computers can be very long and complex. There are
some tricks to speed up the entry process. For example, if an address reads
http://www.teeler.com all you need to really type in is 'teeler' and the
browser assumes the rest. This is the default setting for web browsers, since
most companies use this format for their address.

But why type in the address at all? Usually you can just click on a link
from the page you are visiting, or cut-and-paste the address from an e-mail
message or any other computer document. And to really save time you can
click on one of the buttons on the toolbar: **bookmarks**.

The **bookmarks** file, called **favorites** in *Internet Explorer*, allows you to
create a shortcut from your browser to a specific page within a web site. If
you visit a web page more than two or three times, it is sensible to
'bookmark' it, that is, to flag it for later reference. To do this, click on
Bookmarks and select Add to Bookmarks. This places the address in the
bookmarks file. Later you can edit your file to give the bookmarks
memorable names, file them into separate folders or even automatically
update the addresses that have changed. Bookmarking is a wonderful
feature when you are using the Web with students because you can
bookmark lots of web pages in advance, in a folder labelled with the class's
name. When students come in, they open the bookmarks file, find the
folder for their class and click on the page name to quickly open that page
in the browser.

Another option, Font, allows you to change the appearance of the web
page on your screen. You can make the text larger or smaller by clicking on
Font, which can be really useful if you are working on a small screen.

You can also turn the images off to navigate the Web more quickly. This
is a great money saver because you can load pages more quickly, but it also
takes a lot of the joy out of using the Web.

You can turn the toolbar off (make it disappear) and also the address box
if they are taking up too much of your viewing space, using the Options
menu in *Netscape Navigator* or the View menu in *Internet Explorer*. You
repeat the procedure to make them reappear.

Most of the other features of the toolbar are for navigation. Back and
Forward buttons do just what they say: move one step backwards to where
you have just been, or one step forwards from a page you went back to. But
if you right-click on the same button, a menu drops down to show you all

the places you have visited while online that day. Click on the name of a page in this menu to jump directly to it.

You can also go back to sites you have already visited by clicking on an arrow to the right of the address box (on some browsers), or by clicking on History. This opens the history folder, a record of all the web sites you have visited in the last week or month.

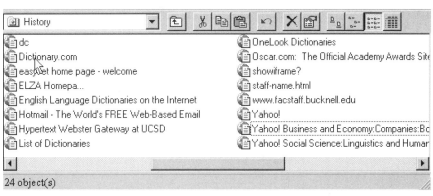

A history folder

Your browser stores, or **caches**, all the web pages you visit in a part of your computer called the cache. This means that when you click on a page in the history folder it loads the page faster because it opens the site directly from the information in the cache first. The cache takes up a lot of space on your computer so your browser empties it periodically to free up memory.

However, sometimes the information on a page from the cache is outdated. When you need to see a newer version of a web page – for example, a newspaper that changes every day – you click the Reload or Refresh button. The browser will now skip the version in the cache and load a fresh copy from the Internet.

The Home button takes you directly back to the web browser's home page. You can change this option easily, and select any web page you like as your default home page – that is, the page that will open automatically each time you connect to the Web.

Details of the specific features of your web browser can be found in the browser's help file, in the drop-down help menu on the toolbar. So if you are using the Web for the first time, you can read through it.

So the toolbar forms the top part of the frame around a web page. The other three sides of the frame are composed of: the scroll bar on the right, which you use to move up and down a page that is too long for your screen; the status bar at the bottom, which tells you what the browser is doing; and a function-less side on the left.

Navigating the Web

Navigating round a web site itself is very easy. It is what is called **point-and-click** technology. You point your mouse at a link and click, which transports you to another page within the web site or to another location altogether.

How do you know if something is a link? The two most common ways are:

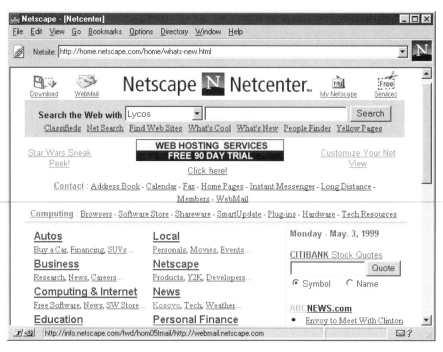

Netscape's *home page*

- **Links** are usually highlighted in a different colour from the rest of the text, and they may be underlined. This system of links is called **hypertext**. When you visit a link it should change colour, to remind you later that you have already seen it.
- If you pass your mouse over different bits of text and pictures the cursor will change, normally from an arrow to a hand. The hand means that you can click there because it is a link. You can tell where the link will take you by watching the address change in the status bar, at the bottom of the browser.

Links can lead to other things as well. You can download software by simply clicking on a link and following the instructions that appear. Links can also be connections to audio and video files, which use special software programs that are integrated into the browser to play them back. These are called helper applications or **plug-ins**, and we take a look at how these work in Chapter 5 (see page 77).

Although the technology is easy, it takes a while to become comfortable with the general format of a web page. You will soon begin to know just where to look for links and how to find the information you need on the page. And as you browse around the Web you will grow familiar with the various styles and designs that are popular, and you will almost certainly run across both extremes of the spectrum: long pages of nearly unformatted text and truly spectacular multimedia extravaganzas.

For many users there is little more to the Internet than this, the ubiquitous Web, with e-mail running a distant second. But there are many other applications besides, some of which are useful to English language teachers. As we examine the different ways the Internet can be used in English language teaching, we will look at a few of these other applications.

Conclusions   In this chapter we have
- tried to define the term 'Internet', separating the series of computer networks that compose the actual highway from the applications that transport information on it. We have outlined the requirements needed to become a member of the online community.
- looked at a brief history of the Internet, and how it has developed into an international communications system.
- described the key text and multimedia applications.
- examined how teachers are using the Internet and viewed results of a study done by the Agora Language Marketplace.
- introduced the basics of e-mail.
- summarised Netiquette, a set of writing conventions for electronic communication.
- dissected a simple web page and analysed the components of a web site address. We have also reviewed some of the most useful features of web browsers and explained how to move between web sites.

Looking ahead
- In the following chapter we will look at using the Net for teacher development, including an overview of mailing lists, newsgroups and real-time communication.
- In Chapter 3, we will take a step-by-step tour through finding the web sites you are interested in.
- We will discuss equipment needs and various alternatives to a traditional telephone connection in Chapter 4.
- Then we will focus on uses for e-mail, multimedia files, and the Web in the classroom in Chapters 5 and 6.

2 The Internet in teacher development

If the Net is the most useful research tool ever available…it is also the most misleading, dangerous and seductive. Every piece of information has to be weighed for possible flaws.
Roger Ebert, 1996

- The Internet as a virtual teachers' room
- The reference library: the World Wide Web
- The cubbyholes: mailing lists
- The noticeboard: newsgroups
- The teachers: chatting and MOOing in cyberspace

The Internet as a virtual teachers' room

Imagine walking into the teachers' room at a new school for the first time. You decide to explore the room and check out what is on offer. One of the first things you notice is an untidy bookcase piled high with reference material. It seems to include just about everything you could possibly need. Apart from the dictionaries, grammar books and other teaching materials there are also several journals and newsletters, a few conference abstracts and research projects, and an assortment of resource books.

Distributed around the room there seem to be lots of cubbyholes labelled with teachers' names, so you wander around until you find yours. There's nothing in it yet, except for a note about the first teachers' meeting. So you move on towards the back wall, where you can see a corkboard covered with notices. You skim over the schedule of training courses available and conference dates coming up. You find a list of job openings and opportunities for career advancement, some notes about lesson plans, comments on new materials received, requests for research partners and what looks like an advertisement for a local bookshop.

Every so often a group of teachers walk into the room and start talking. They could be discussing their latest lesson, a great lesson idea, problems with the present perfect, doubts about assessment or tips for managing young learners. They could just be talking about what to have for lunch. They wander in and out, chatting, as you ramble around the room. Maybe you just hang around a while, listening as you get accustomed to your new surroundings. Or perhaps you jump right in and introduce yourself, ask a question or put in your two-cents' worth.

'Wait a minute!' you exclaim. 'My teachers' room looks nothing like that. Where have you been teaching?'

Yes, true enough. The well-stocked teachers' room can be a powerful development tool, but unfortunately, too many teachers find themselves without one. In that case, what options are available for those who lack the comprehensive reference library, the overflowing noticeboards, the helpful colleagues?

Let's go back into the ideal teachers' room for a moment. Expand that room so that you have infinitely more space for materials, a boundless arena for discussion and an endless source of up-to-date news – in short, you have the Internet. The Internet allows teaching professionals almost instant access to a vast amount of reference material, but even more than that, it lets us contact each other with the push of a button – whether the other person is just down the road or halfway around the world. And no one has to come in to dust it.

The cluttered reference library has been transformed into the **World Wide Web**. The familiar cubbyholes are now your **e-mail** system. The overflowing noticeboards have become **mailing lists** and **newsgroups**. The teachers are still there – present in the chat rooms and virtual conferences regularly organised by various groups. So let's take a closer look at this virtual teachers' room.

The reference library: the World Wide Web

The World Wide Web is fast becoming the largest reference library in the world. What started out as a very specialised resource now encompasses just about every topic known to man. Not only can you take information from it, but you can also contribute to it and get involved by starting a web site of your own. You might publish your thesis, latest research findings or practical classroom ideas for the world to read and respond to. The Web is constantly changing, adapting and expanding at such a rate that it is impossible to maintain an index for it. Luckily, there are gateway sites.

Gateway sites

Gateways are basically **web sites** with lists of links to other resource sites, as well as superb material of their own. They frequently offer tips on how to use the Internet and advice on searching the Web for what you need. The gateways for English language teachers are maintained by organisations and individuals who dedicate a lot of time to finding useful resources on the Web, and then categorising and updating links to them so that you do not have to reinvent the wheel every time you open your web **browser**. *Dave Sperling's ESL Cafe* (see page 18) is one of these gateway sites. It is updated regularly and should be a frequent stopover on your travels around the Internet. You will find a list of gateway web sites in Appendix D on page 110.

Professional associations

How do you keep up with your local, regional or international teachers' association? One answer could be by looking at their web site (such as the JALT web site on page 18). More and more teaching organisations are joining the **online** community every day: and that is a lot of teachers.

On a web site of this kind you might find an updated list of speakers or the latest schedule changes for a forthcoming event. Some sites allow you to

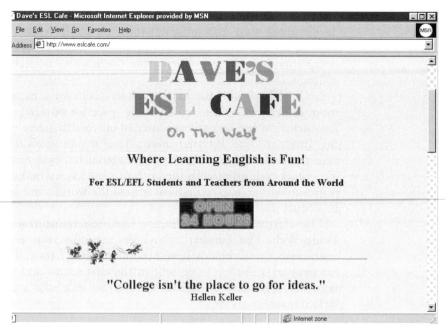

A gateway site: Dave Sperling's ESL Cafe

This is the home page for JALT (the Japan Association for Language Teaching)

print out proposal forms or even fill out a special form right on the screen. And they let you contact the association with the click of a button, day or night, all year round – taking into account the human factor at the other end, of course.

The Web makes it possible for conference organisers to link their site to relevant information such as city and transport maps, lists of hotels and restaurants, information about speakers, related articles and exhibitors' sites: information that would have been prohibitively expensive to send out to individual conference participants, and that may have arrived too late to be of any use.

Increasingly, conference organisers are offering some type of **virtual** participation for those who are unable to attend in person. This may take the form of an online programme with abstracts of presentations. It might include interviews with participants about sessions they have attended or summaries of talks with the speakers' handouts. And for those fortunate enough to have **videoconferencing** capabilities, this kind of 'virtual' participation could grant entire teaching communities at least partial access to events happening on the other side of the world.

Most web sites are also designed to give as much helpful information about the organisation as possible, and to allow you to get in touch with the association itself, if only by giving a contact name and e-mail address.

Journals and newsletters

Academic publications are another tremendous resource of the online community. You will find extensive listings of paper publications that you can subscribe to, in the traditional sense of the word 'subscribe'. But many professional journals and newsletters also offer selections from their latest issue over the Web. Some provide supplementary material to complement the contents of the paper copy. Others – such as the *TESL EJ* – only exist online.

Let's have a look at how you might use online publications to research a topic. Say you were thinking of signing up for a course on Neuro-Linguistic Programming (NLP). Before you enrol you would like to know a little more about the subject, but it is midnight and the library has been closed for hours. So you turn on your computer, connect to the Web and search for articles on NLP (see pages 37–49 for how to search for information).

What might you find? Keeping in mind that the content of the Internet changes daily, here is a taste of what might be available at any given time:

- *JALT Newsletter*, February 1997 special NLP issue
- *Merl's World of NLP*: frequently asked questions
- Neurolinguistic Programming: *The Skeptic's Dictionary* definition
- *NLP Information* interactive site

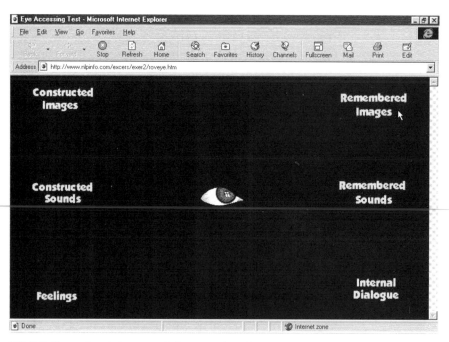

NLP Information *is just one of the many sites that may be listed as an NLP site. Here you can see their interactive roving eye page*

Academic databases

There are many documents available from academic **database** sites as well. For example, *The ERIC Digest*, from the Educational Resources Information Centre, is now available on the Web. Its primary goal is to improve education in the United States, but ERIC defines its audience as everyone related to education, and provides a vast database of educational research and articles on the many topics related to teaching, learning and educational decision making. There is a special section dedicated to CAL: the Centre for Applied Linguistics.

Web browsers make it easy to access sites such as *CELIA*, the database at La Trobe University in Australia. These are not really web sites at all, but employ an earlier, less user-friendly Internet system – called **FTP** or **File Transfer Protocol** – to send documents and other files to your computer. If you click on a link to one of the documents from within your web browser you will notice that the address begins with **ftp:** rather than **http:**. Your browser should automatically accept that address, so you do not need to have special software to access these files.

Distance-learning courses and schools

While distance learning has been around for ages, the Internet may have changed the face of the medium forever. It makes sense really. From the moment you decide you would like to continue your education, the Internet can provide access to detailed information about the many institutions and distance-learning courses currently available to you worldwide – information about the teachers, deadlines, grants and fees. Clearly, this is faster and more convenient than 'traditional' methods of finding the same information. And while some sites confine themselves to offering basic course catalogues and enrolment forms, others present a much fuller picture.

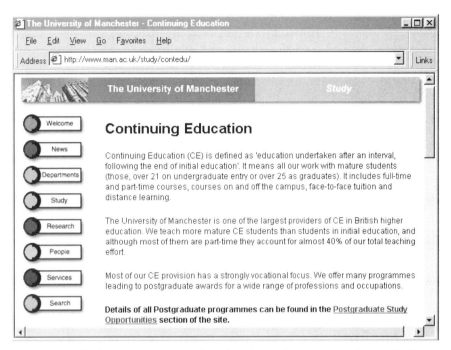

An example of information on continuing education and distance learning available on the University of Manchester *site*

Courses can also capitalise on the ease of publishing on the Web. A course web site might include a syllabus, a summary of lessons, notes, links to helpful sites and related research, projects done by students, model assignments and a long list of etceteras considered impractical under the more traditional system. The interactivity of the Web allows for spontaneous feedback and rapid change, without the hassle of endless photocopying.

During the course of your studies, many different **applications** of the Internet may be used. For example, distance-learning courses now customarily take advantage of the speed of basic e-mail to forward reading lists, assignments and course support materials. Communication with the course instructor is more efficient this way and questions can be handled more swiftly. Contact between classmates becomes feasible, making group tasks and project work real options for the isolated distance learner. Here again, videoconferencing is becoming much more common as the technology becomes available to the general population. More personal, face-to-face discussion with tutors or classmates is now a real possibility.

It should also be much easier for you to stay in contact and keep abreast of developments after the course ends. Post-course support and follow-up can take place via **discussion boards** or **mailing lists** at your convenience. So check out what the school offers by way of follow-up support before you sign up for a course.

Other resources on the Web

- **Information for research**: Planning a new research project has become far less tedious with the expansion of the Internet. By searching the databases and web sites you can determine what projects are currently underway, find international research partners or just simply read up on your subject.
- **Practical classroom ideas**: Whether you are looking for grammar-based or topical material, you will probably find something that fits the bill. The secret lies in finding it quickly, and knowing how to adapt it for your students. Discussion of these procedures is covered in Chapter 3 (see pages 36–53).
- **Publishers**: As the Web makes room for commercial sites, more and more publishers are starting to maintain booklists and to promote new publications and authors on their web sites. Many offer tips for teachers and information about forthcoming presentations and workshops. At the last count there were more than 200 such sites available.
- **Online dictionaries, grammars and encyclopaedias**: Many of the classic reference books are available on the Web. You can even have a direct link to your favourite online dictionary from your **desktop**. And a reference work that would be unwieldy if printed becomes a handy resource on the Web. Then there are reference sites that push the technology to its limits – such as *Plumb Design's Visual Thesaurus*: an interactive mindmap for discovering vocabulary, 'an exploration of the sense relationships within the English language' (illustrated on page 66).
- **Grants and scholarships**: Whether you are looking for a government endowment, international travel grant, funding for a conference or a specific award or scholarship, the Internet is the perfect place to start. Data are updated regularly, so you have the latest information at your fingertips when you need it, before the application deadline has passed.
- **Career advancement**: Recruitment and employment information is available from a variety of sources, but there are several reasons to investigate the job listings on the Web. They are international, so they offer a broader field of operations, and they provide up-to-the-minute listings. Dedicated sites focusing on ELT allow you to search for jobs relating to your special skills more easily. They ease the application process, too, by offering clickable links for more detailed inquiries.

One interesting site that has made its way onto the Web is the *Electronic JobShop* provided by the International Association of Teachers of English as a Foreign Language (IATEFL). This natural extension of the IATEFL annual conference jobshop is updated weekly, and is run as part of the Digital Education Network (DEN) alongside the *ELT Job Centre*.

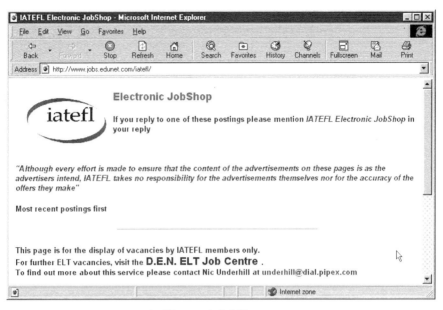

The home page of the IATEFL Electronic JobShop

The cubbyholes: mailing lists

Once you are comfortable using your e-mail program, and you are familiar with the rules of **Netiquette**, you are ready to join your first mailing list.

Mailing lists, or 'lists', are basically e-mail discussion groups focusing on a single theme. A group of people with a common interest decide they would like to communicate with each other on a regular basis by e-mail. So they contact a computer expert, who sets up a program on a powerful computer somewhere: a mailing list program. Now all the others have to do is send the computer program their name and e-mail address to **subscribe** to the new list. From then on, any time one of them sends a message to the list, everyone in the group receives the same message in their mailbox to read and reply to as they wish. New subscribers can join the discussion list at any time.

New lists often start out quite small, but grow quickly as others hear about the discussion and join in. Mailing lists are an inexpensive, convenient way to keep in touch with others, so new lists are starting all the time. There are almost as many different lists as there are teachers. Each list is targeted at a different sector of the community. Many teachers' associations, both international and regional, have lists to discuss the concerns of their members, and give up-to-the-minute news on conferences and workshops, calls for papers and publications. And of course, there are lists for almost every subject imaginable: applied linguistics, second language acquisition, testing, skills work, ESP, etc. You will find an abridged directory of current ELT mailing lists in Appendix C on page 109 to start you off.

One caveat, however – the quality of the interaction depends entirely on the list participants. Experiment with a few to find the ones that are most interesting. Most e-mail discussion groups for English language teachers are relatively free from the problems that you might encounter in non-academic areas of the Internet.

Subscribing to *TESL-L*

In order to explain how lists work in more detail we will look at one of the most popular lists for ELT: *TESL-L*, a 24-hour electronic resource for anyone interested in the teaching of the English language. Physically located in New York, in a recent count *TESL-L* linked over 20,000 virtual subscribers in 125 countries. This resource is freely available worldwide to anyone with access to an e-mail account.

To subscribe, just send this e-mail message from your address to the list address: SUB TESL-L your name

You must leave the subject line of the message BLANK, and turn your signature OFF. If you have made a mistake, the computer at the other end will usually send you a message to tell you what you did wrong. It's an automated reply from a computer, so just try again.

An e-mail message asking to subscribe to TESL-L

Once you are a subscriber the messages come to you automatically. You receive information about conferences, job openings, methodology, grammar, and teaching ideas. You can communicate your concerns to your virtual colleagues around the world. It is very much like a real teachers' room in that way – sometimes teachers know the answers to your queries, sometimes they don't; often they are interested in what you are saying and reply, and at other times they may skip over your message altogether.

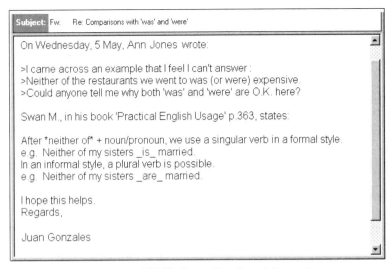

Subject: Fw: Re: Comparisons with 'was' and 'were'

On Wednesday, 5 May, Ann Jones wrote:

>I came across an example that I feel I can't answer :
>Neither of the restaurants we went to was (or were) expensive.
>Could anyone tell me why both 'was' and 'were' are O.K. here?

Swan M., in his book 'Practical English Usage' p.363, states:

After *neither of* + noun/pronoun, we use a singular verb in a formal style.
e.g. Neither of my sisters _is_ married.
In an informal style, a plural verb is possible.
e.g. Neither of my sisters _are_ married.

I hope this helps.
Regards,

Juan Gonzales

A sample message from the TESL-L *mailing list with a reply*

New users of the Internet often '**lurk**' for a time, reading messages without replying or posting any messages of their own. This is an excellent way to get to know the interests of the group and to feel more self-confident about taking that first step. In fact, the first message you receive from a list should be a welcome message with a few tips to get you started.

To get the most out of your mailing list experience remember three things: mind your Netiquette, avoid **cross-posting** and make sure you send personal replies to the appropriate individual's address, not to the entire list.

One nice thing about *TESL-L* is that it is has a human administrator who limits the number of messages that go out on any one day. This person also checks the messages for relevance to the list, which is one of the reasons this list can be a good one to choose.

Managing your list messages

Managing your messages from a mailing list can become a time-consuming task. You may find you are receiving far too many each day. Some might be irrelevant to your situation, or personal replies to someone else. Mailing lists offer you several options that can simplify this chore.

- **Digest**: First you can request a 'digest' of all the messages. This means that you will receive a single e-mail message containing all the messages sent out that day - a faster option for those worried about the telephone bill. One message is also a bit easier to file.
- **Index**: For even faster retrieval you can request the 'index' option. That way you will just get a list of available messages for

that day. If you are interested in reading a particular message, you will need to send a message to the *TESL-L* computer asking for that message by number. It will then be e-mailed to you.

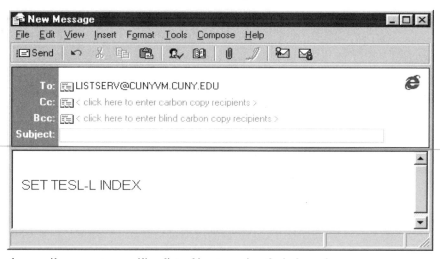

An e-mail message to a mailing list asking to receive the index only

- **Archive**: You can check the list archives before posting a new message to see what has already been discussed. This will keep you from receiving angry replies from long-time list members. *TESL-L* has a huge archive including many papers, articles, and bibliographies. There are also collections of discussions sorted by topic, and even some lesson plans and teaching materials.
- **Nomail**: When you go away you can request that no messages be sent to you until further notice. That way your in-box is not stuffed with mail when you get back. This can be exceedingly important for people whose service provider limits the number of messages they can have waiting. CompuServe and other **ISPs** usually limit the number to 100, so if that crucial message from the bank is number 101, it gets 'returned to sender'. This is also a useful option for teachers who do not have time to read through all the messages on a regular basis, but who would still like to be able to reply to an interesting message on occasion.

    Another benefit of the Nomail option is that you can read the messages in the mailing list's corresponding **newsgroup**, if there is one. (Newsgroups are described in the next section.) This means that you do not have to download all the messages from the list every day.
- **Mail**: When you return, you just ask for mail to begin by sending another message. You might check the index to see if you missed any really exciting discussion while you were away.
- **FAQ**: You can usually access a collection of frequently asked questions (FAQs). This saves you from having to wait for a reply, and keeps the administrators from tearing their hair out after answering the same question for the umpteenth time. Check through your welcome message and FAQs before sending in that question.

To set any of the options, you send a message to the list computer. The e-mail address should be the same one you subscribed to, and you should be able to find it again by scanning the welcome message. You will receive an automated reply, giving your current settings for that list.

Finding lists on other topics

It is likely that you will want to expand your horizons outside the confines of the ELT circuit, or at least beyond the boundaries of the abridged list of lists contained in this book. You may need to search for mailing lists related to a certain topic, so a visit to *Tile.net* or *Liszt* should be your next stop. Both are directories of the literally tens of thousands of lists currently operating.

Liszt is a subject-based directory, which gives you a set of categories to choose from. That means it may be a bit easier to start with, if you are not sure exactly what you are looking for. It has a database of 85,000 lists.

Tile.net lets you search alphabetically, by topic or by author. It has fewer lists in its directory, but besides informing you of the list's name and address, *Tile.net* tells you how many people are subscribed, where the list is situated, and how to contact the administrator of the list.

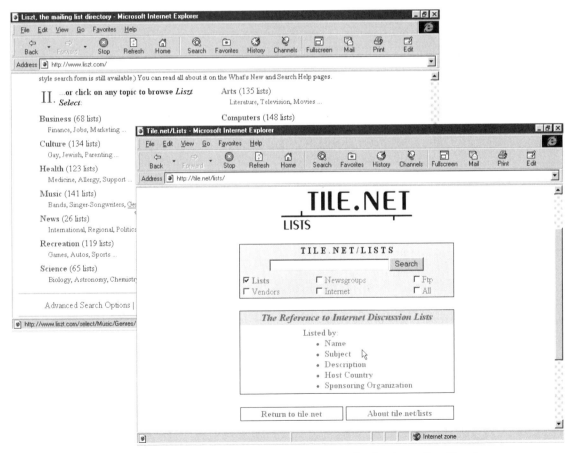

Liszt *and* Tile.net *are two web sites that offer databases of mailing lists*

To use *Liszt* you start by clicking on the category you think will contain information on lists for your topic. Let's say you were looking for a list about the Blues. You might click on the link to 'music – genres', which will take you to a further set of subcategories. In 'genres', we click on 'blues' and there it is, '*BLUES-L*: The Blues Music List'.

Tile.net is quite similar. To find the same list as above, just click on 'subject', then 'music'. This takes you straight to a long list of mailing lists associated with music of all kinds. *BLUES-L* is seventh on this alphabetised index.

Leaving a mailing list

The most common mistake people make when they want to delete their address from a mailing list is to send a message to the list itself, so everyone but the computer they wish to communicate with ends up reading their note. So first, check the welcome message for the original e-mail address; the one that you subscribed to. Then send the unsubscribe message, NO subject, NO signature. You should receive an automated reply telling you that your message was received successfully.

And that is all there is to it. Mailing lists are really just a 'drop in the bucket' of professional resources available to the English language teacher and teacher trainer. They are, however, accessible to almost everyone, regardless of your computer system or previous experience with computers.

The noticeboard: newsgroups

No, **newsgroups** have nothing to do with the news media in the traditional sense. They are networks of useful discussion forums that are openly accessible over the Internet rather than through the e-mail system, and are vehicles for the redistribution of some mailing lists.

The academic network – called Bitnet – houses several academic discussion groups as well as duplicates of some of the mailing lists we looked at above. This can be a faster, cheaper way to keep up with these mailing lists because you download only the messages you are interested in – at your convenience. And you no longer have to worry about setting the mailing list options to manage messages when you go away for a few weeks. You do not even have to subscribe to the original mailing list to respond to a newsgroup message. However, if you are not a subscriber you cannot send replies to everyone on the list.

The format of the messages is a bit different, with messages arranged according to their subject heading, called the 'thread'. This makes it easy to review comments others have made on the same topic before replying or asking a question of your own. But it is important to remember that newsgroup messages are permanently available over the Internet for everyone to read rather than in your private e-mail account.

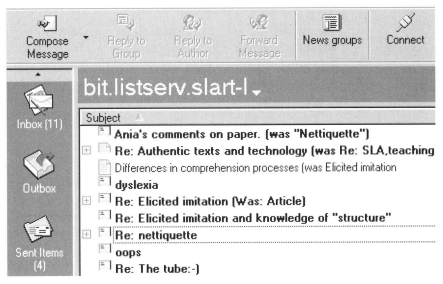

An example message list from SLART-L, *the Second Language Acquisition Research List at:* bit.listserv.slart-l

The general newsgroup network – or **Usenet** – is home to roughly 28,000 other discussion forums on assorted topics. As with mailing lists, some groups are **moderated** – refereed or regulated by someone – but most are not, so silliness abounds. This is not to say that all unmoderated newsgroups are worthless as far as teacher development is concerned. There are some fascinating discussions taking place out there, but their quality depends entirely on the interests of the current participants.

What do the names mean?

Newsgroups are organised into very broad categories, which are then sorted into subcategories, so the names look quite complicated to start with. Like e-mail addresses, newsgroup names are divided by 'dots'. If we dissect one of the names it might be slightly easier to follow what that means.

bit.listserv.slart-l	*bit*	is the general category. In this case Bitnet, the academic network
	listserv	is the subcategory, here a computer automated mailing program
	slart-l	is the specific group, the name of the original mailing list

See Appendix B (page 108) for further information about some newsgroup categories that may be relevant to ELT.

How do newsgroups work?

Newsgroups do not send e-mail to your mailbox. Instead, the messages are kept on the newsgroup's computer until you are ready to read them. To read newsgroups, you will need to have two things:

- **Newsreader**: This is a software program that runs on your computer, allowing you to subscribe to newsgroups and view their messages. The best individual newsreader programs available might be *Newswatcher* for Mac-users and *Free Agent* or *Gravity* for PCs. These programs are available from the Internet as needed, once you are online. But web browsers such as the ones we looked at in Chapter 1 often include a **newsreader** with their other options, so there is usually no need to look for an individual software application.

- **News server**: A **news server** is a program that runs on a remote computer and delivers current newsgroup messages via the Internet to your computer when you decide to read them. All you need to know is the name of the news server to type into the appropriate place in the newsreader set-up. Your ISP should be able to tell you which news server they use to provide access to newsgroups. This information will be very important when you are configuring your newsreader, so write it down somewhere safe. However you may find that you do not need to do this, but can simply click on a Read news icon or News server folder within your e-mail program, to call up the list of newsgroups your ISP gives access to.

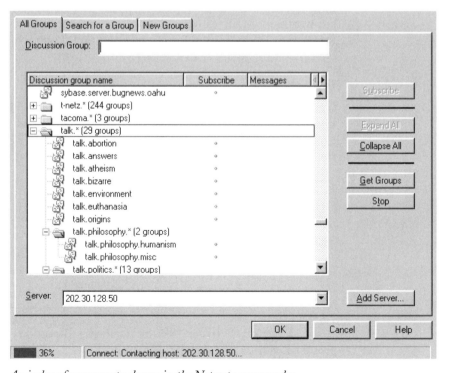

An index of newsgroups shown in the Netscape newsreader

Finding newsgroups

The first step in choosing a newsgroup to subscribe to is finding out which **newsgroups** are available on your **news server**. Use your **newsreader** to view an index of these. (They will be listed by category.) For descriptions of particular newsgroups, look at the *Tile.net* site, which carries details of newsgroups as well as mailing lists.

Some news servers provide only a limited selection of newsgroups. If you have heard of a newsgroup that you would like to join, but do not see it listed in your news server's index, you do not have to use the specific news server provided by your ISP. You can quite easily change to one of the news servers freely available on the Internet, which you can find by searching the Web for 'Public Access News Servers' (see Chapter 3).

Subscribing to newsgroups is usually quite simple: click on the name of the newsgroup and then on the command Subscribe. Request a list of new messages available from that newsgroup, following the instructions for your newsreader. Once you have this list, select the messages that interest you. To read them, download them from the server by highlighting them and clicking on the command Download selected messages. This may take several minutes, while your computer connects and retrieves the files. But then you can disconnect and read them at your leisure.

The teachers: chatting and MOOing in cyberspace

Teachers are all around the Internet. They are present in each and every one of the areas we have already looked at, but in a time-delayed way, like messages left on an answering machine. This is useful technology, and yet, there are times when you just really need to talk to that person live.

Chat programs

This is where '**real-time**' or synchronous technology comes in. Maybe you have heard of 'chat' software, or **IRC**. IRC stands for Internet Relay Chat. It should really be Internet Relay Type, since you are using your keyboard to type out what you would like to say. Communication this way is heavily dependent on your typing skills. Messages can come fast and furious, and the chat environment could be said to have a language all its own. But don't let that put you off. This is one of the most popular areas of the Internet.

Chat is basically a number of people typing simultaneously, reading and replying to what others in their group or **channel** are saying. In a way it is like e-mail, but more expensive because you must be **online** while you are chatting. As you can see from the screen overleaf, names, commands and chat are all mixed up together. Using this kind of chat calls for plenty of practice, so there are special '**newbie**' – or new user – chat areas as well.

Like newsgroups, chat requires special software. You can download this software from many sites on the Internet. Be sure to get the right software for your computer: for example, mIRC for PCs, and Ircle for the Mac, are examples of basic chat software. Once you have installed the software, you will need to set it up, and connect to an IRC **server**. (This is similar to the news server described on page 30.) If in doubt, contact your service provider for help.

```
> excuse me, back in a few minutes (your English is great) - I'll be back
[16:50]   *** jjonddon (~jjonddon@210.120.14.133) has joined #englearn
[16:50]   <joandarc> just went to english courses and schools of english when I was younger
[16:50]   <bcostello> hi jjonddon!
[16:50]   <jjonddon> hello
[16:51]   <bcostello> Are you still studying English?
[16:51]   <joanadarc> hi, JJ
[16:51]   <jjonddon> thanks
[16:51]   <jjonddon> thanks
[16:51]   <joanadarc> No...I learn quite a lot here at Mirc
[16:51]   <bcostello> The film I saw was "La Tieta do Agrieste"
[16:51]   <joanadarc> Are u a teacher?
[16:51]   <bcostello> Where are u from jj?
[16:52]   <joanadarc> How did u like it??
[16:52]   <jjonddon> korea
[16:52]   <bcostello> Yes, I admit it. I'm a teacher.
[16:52]   <bcostello> What time is it in Korea now?
[16:52]   <jjonddon> am 00:53
[16:52]   <joanadarc> Its 12:52 in Sao Paulo
[16:52]   <bcostello> I liked the film a lot, jo - great music
[16:53]   <joanadarc> I havent seen it but I love the music too. I like Caetano Veloso
[16:53]   <bcostello> Do you study English jj?
[16:53]   <jjonddon> yes..
[16:54]   <jjonddon> I am poor English
[16:54]   <bcostello> After I saw the film I really wanted to visit Brasil
[16:54]   <joanadarc> Where r u from, Costello?
[16:54]   <joanadarc> Why dont you come over here?
[16:54]   <bcostello> Don't worry jj, just say what you want
[16:54]   <jjonddon> how?
> Sorry people I have to go - nice talking to you all
[16:55]   <joanadarc> JJ, whats your job?
```

This chat channel for students and teachers of English around the world is run by International House in Barcelona

Not unlike newsgroups, each chat area has a name, which is called a channel. There are channels about, well, just about everything. You can find out what channels are available by clicking on the List channels button, or by typing the command **/list** in the **text box**. If you double-click on a channel name you will join in the conversation on that channel, and a list of other participants automatically appears in a column on the right. Find one channel you like, and get other teachers to join in at the same time. You can then have an instant conference.

Learning to use chat programs means spending a certain amount of time experimenting. This is no longer the realm of **point-and-click**. Chat programs use typed commands, and specific jargon. Some are more intuitive and user-friendly than others. **ICQ** (sound the name out) is a very good example; it is great for new users and perhaps more adaptable to teacher development purposes. Each ICQ user receives an ID number, similar to a telephone number. You can use these numbers to set up a list of contacts. Then the program automatically notifies you when anyone on the list connects. It also has private chat rooms so that you can arrange meetings with other users.

Attempts to make chat programs more appealing have led to chat systems with graphics and images. So you can now meet people in different worlds, such as in a virtual space station. In these chat worlds, you are represented by a sort of animated character, called an 'avatar'. 'Avatar chat' is in fact a good search term to use when looking for virtual chat sites. (For more on searches see pages 37–49.)

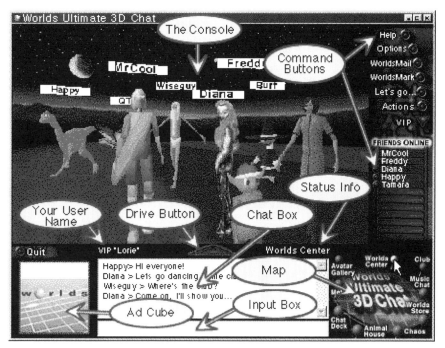

A page from Worlds Chat, *a virtual chat site*

MOO virtual environments

MOO stands for 'multi-user object-oriented dimension'. Try to imagine a MOO as a place, a permanent space on the Internet set aside for a specific group, a virtual environment. Perhaps you could call it an online community because there is a sense of community in a MOO that does not exist elsewhere on the Net.

MOOs are called 'object-oriented' because objects form a key part of the experience but, as in literature, only words are used to describe the objects. There are no illustrations. Objects that you come across in a MOO might be: people; things, like a book; places, like a park or a cafe; a small computer program, such as a virtual taxi or even a game of Scrabble.

The difference between visiting a MOO and reading a text is that you can interact with the objects. Even if no one else is in the MOO, you can wander around the 'place' and 'look' at these objects – well, read them anyway. And when someone 'walks in' you can talk to them in **real time**. You 'move' around the rooms and buildings by typing in commands. This takes a while to get used to, and can be a bit daunting to start out with. What makes MOOs different from chat programs is the sense of community, of permanence. MOOs can also be quite supportive environments: you can usually ask anyone there to give you a hand when you begin to feel a bit lost.

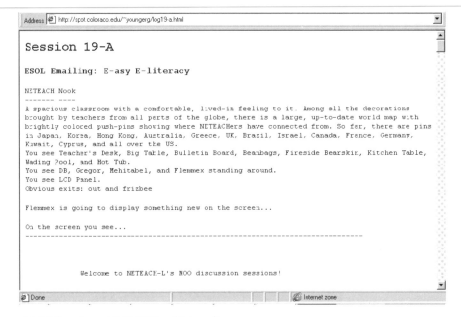

A MOO session at SchMOOze University

Since April 1996, the people at *NETEACH-L* have been hosting MOOing sessions at SchMOOze University. SchMOOze is a MOO with an ELT focus, which gives students a friendly location to practise their English. It is also an excellent place to meet other teachers new to MOOs who are interested in their application to English teaching. A 'MOO master' co-ordinates the *NETEACH-L* biweekly teacher discussions there. A schedule of these meetings is available from their web site.

The *NETEACH-L* web site also offers an introductory list of commands to get you started, and archives of list messages related to MOOing. It is great to be able to read through other people's experiences with the technology before actually trying it yourself. There are many other web sites that offer advice on how to get started using MOOs, and how to get the necessary software for your system. Read though these guidelines and you can practise before you get involved in the real thing.

You may be getting e-mail messages by now, telling you to meet a group of teachers in a certain place at a certain time for a virtual conference. This is your invitation to the world of MOOing, perhaps one of the most underrated tools on the Internet as far as instant communication goes. MOOs are also perfect places to hold virtual conferences for teacher training. International organisations have started using MOOs to allow people who cannot physically attend to participate in conferences from the comfort of their own schools.

That ends our quick tour of the Internet Virtual Teachers' Room. Remember, we've only skimmed the surface of what is out there.

Conclusions

In this chapter we have
- looked at how English language teachers can use the World Wide Web as a reference library for continuing development.
- discussed the benefits of joining mailing lists.
- outlined techniques for subscribing to mailing lists and managing messages, and suggested two databases to search for lists by topic.
- introduced newsgroups, which are useful discussion forums in their own right, but also offer an alternative method of accessing mailing lists.
- talked about the advantages and disadvantages of using real-time communication technology such as Internet Relay Chat.
- Described the multi-user environments called MOOs, and considered their possible use for teacher development.

Looking ahead

- In the next chapter we will look at using the Internet as a materials resource, and suggest techniques for searching the Internet for materials and adapting them once you find them.

3 The Internet as a materials resource

Give a man a fish and you feed him for a day; teach him to use the Net and he won't bother you for weeks.
Anonymous

- Why use the Internet for materials?
- Some issues to consider
- Finding ELT materials: using gateways and Webrings
- Expanding your search: using browsers, directories and search engines
- What is a metasearch?
- Searching in the future
- Adapting Internet materials
- Copyright and the Internet

Why use the Internet for materials?

The Internet has several advantages as a source of teaching materials:

- **Scope**: How big is the Internet? Huge might be the most exact answer – though computer scientists at the NEC Research Institute in the United States estimate that as of April 1998 there were over 320 million pages. As a vast virtual library the Internet offers a seemingly endless range of topics to choose from, all in one handy location. There are even a growing number of materials specifically designed for English language teaching. It is a paperless medium and so it escapes the size restrictions that are characteristic of the coursebook. Internet files *do* have a tangible volume, but the limitations in scope are determined by the users' speed of access and the computer facilities available.

- **Topicality**: While some of the content of the Internet is several years old, much of it is updated on a regular basis: monthly, weekly or daily. You can get today's news from any number of publications without buying them all in the hope of finding that one useful item. And of course, many new publications are being added every day, some of them unavailable in print.

- **Personalisation**: Coursebooks are inescapably limited by the magnitude of the audience for which they are written. The topics they deal with may be irrelevant or difficult to discuss with your class, and you may sometimes need alternative topics and texts. The Internet can greatly simplify the task of finding them.

Some issues to consider

At times, however, the Internet seems more like a boundless filing cabinet than a library. When a filing cabinet is brand new it is obviously quite easy to sort the files. But as time passes, papers accumulate and the cabinet may become a catch-all for scraps of paper, cuttings from the newspaper and a lost sock or two. In the early stages of its evolution, finding material on the Internet was also a simple matter. You could ring a colleague, who made a call to a friend that knew the exact name of the file you needed. Then you just typed those instructions into your computer to retrieve the desired information.

Now there are over 20 million addresses in this virtual filing system and this has led to some difficulties. Foremost of these is the lack of a comprehensive index. The speed at which the Internet changes, and the roughly 125,000 additional domain names registered each month, make such an index quite impossible. This must be the reason that thirteen of the top twenty web sites in the *Web 21* popularity rankings are actually search mechanisms of one kind or another. In order to save valuable time it is especially important to understand the ins-and-outs of the search tools that are available to you. Deciding how to search is at least as important as the search process itself, so in the next few sections we will take an in-depth look at techniques for searching the Internet.

Another problem is that many schools do not yet have the facilities that would allow classes direct access to the Internet. Even teachers may have restricted access because of the costs involved or the logistics of scheduling. An easy solution to the problem of limited access is to print materials from the Net and give the printed sheets to students.

But the above 'solution' may not always be appropriate because of another key feature of the Internet, namely that most of the material on it has not been produced for learners of English.

- The authors of much of the material available are native speakers of English and as such they are apt to use idiomatic expressions. These may sometimes be difficult, or even unsuitable, to use in the classroom.
- Language may contain grammatical errors and information presented can be completely inaccurate.
- The design can be extremely dense and forbidding, or just plain boring.

It is important to look at Net materials as closely as you would at materials from any other source, and where necessary take the time to adapt them to suit your situation. Later in this chapter we will discuss how to adapt Internet texts, within the laws of copyright, so that these can then be presented to students as print-outs or on-screen.

First, however, let's take a look at how to find the materials.

Finding ELT materials: using gateways and Webrings

Finding materials designed specifically for ELT – because they are still so limited in number – is considerably easier than locating authentic materials on a particular topic. If your goal is to find lesson plans, quizzes and other related activities, an excellent place to begin your search is at one of the **gateway sites** described in Chapter 2 (see page 17).

Another trusty starting point is the **Webring**, which differs from a gateway in one important particular: you do not have to keep returning to the first list of sites, but are able to travel in a circle around the ring. The main web site features a list of thematically based groups, the rings, each of which is a series of interrelated sites. There are rings linking lesson plans for home study, foreign language education sites, educational sites by age group, etc.

The Webring most suited to ELT is called the *ESLoop*. Among the 90 different sites on this Webring you can find student activities, academic papers, ESP materials and job opportunities. Each site is linked to the next, so that you can move in a linear path through all the sites, or choose to view sites in a random order.

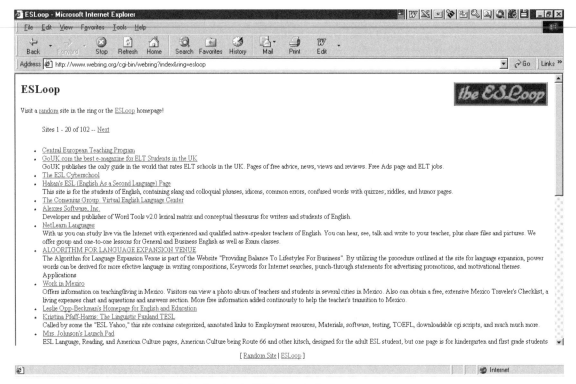

A few of the sites in the ESLoop *index*

Expanding your search: using browsers, directories and search engines

There are thousands of search tools on the Net. Some are comprehensive, while some are very specialist tools. To begin any search for authentic materials you should have a clear idea of what you are looking for. Are you pursuing a celebrity photo, an airline timetable, the latest sports results or a text to practise the present perfect? This in itself may determine the best tool to use for your research.

And while using the right tool will certainly better your odds, no one mode of searching is flawless. No single search mechanism can ferret out more than a third of the available information. Net gurus often suggest using a combination of the following search methods to get fuller, more comprehensive results. Patience, flexibility and lateral thinking can also help.

Browsers: a quick search

In many cases, the easiest way to begin is right on your web browser's toolbar.

- Clicking the Search icon will lead you to a more-than-adequate search tool, linked to your browser's home page. However, because most of the millions of Internet users work with one of the two popular browsers these search pages are among the most overcrowded sites on the Web.
- Using the address box on the toolbar is a much quicker way to get the same information. By typing the command Go... in the address box, together with your topic or **keyword**, you send a precise request for information directly to the browser search mechanism, bypassing that bustling home page. The word Find... can be used in the same way.

An example of using the command: Go

This class of search will bring you only a modest number of results, so it is most convenient for hunting for something you are certain exists but whose exact address you do not know.

Directories: the human element

Directories, or hierarchical indices, are user-friendly places to initiate a search, especially if you are testing the waters for the first time. There are no special skills needed to use this type of search tool, which is basically a database of selected web site addresses that have been divided into helpful categories. These categories are then further divided into subcategories and so on, until there are no further possible divisions.

Directories use an indexing strategy that makes them distinct from other search tools. They use real live people to search the Web, and to review and categorise the sites by topic. This reduces some of the aggravations that frequently plague the researcher, such as duplication of listings, broken links and out-of-date information. A perfect choice when you have very little idea what is out there, directories are set up to satisfy expert and inexperienced users alike. This is why *Yahoo!*, one of the pioneer **directory** sites, is consistently ranked number one in Internet polls.

How to use a directory

To search with a directory such as *Yahoo!* just type the address of the directory you want to use in your browser's address box. When the site opens, click on one of the categories or subheadings. This will take you to the category, where there are lists of subcategories, which you can click on. You bore down, level by level, until you find the information you are seeking.

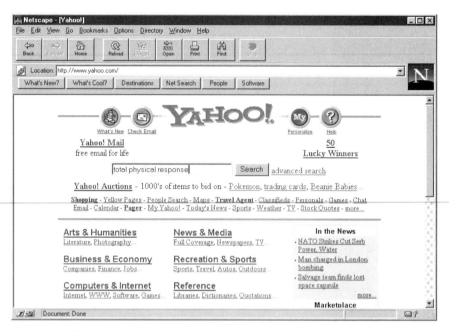

The popular Yahoo! *directory has various international editions and has a special version for children*

Each category also provides, below the list of subcategories, a list of relevant web sites. You can click on these to go directly to these sites. If a site is not all that you were hoping for, just click on your browser's Back button to return to the last *Yahoo!* page you visited.

Another way to search a directory is by typing keywords into the white box next to the search button, the search box. Choosing your keywords carefully makes your search much more efficient. For example, if you type 'London' in the box, *Yahoo!* will find all the categories and web pages that relate to that city in any way. But if you specify 'London theatre', the results you get back are more likely to be about theatre in London.

Spelling is clearly important. Consider the regional variations ('theater' or 'theatre') and word forms (singular or plural, noun or verb) that might get more results from the directory. It is possible to account for this – in part – by typing the word stem followed by an asterisk (theat*). This asks the directory to search for all the various words with the specified stem ('theatre', 'theaters', 'theatrical').

Underneath the search box you will find a couple of options for your query: to search the entire *Yahoo!* database or to search only in the category that you have chosen. Just click in the white circle, or radio button, next to the option you wish to select. Then click on the Search button to send in your query. If you have been at it for quite a while, without success, then perhaps it would be best to choose the All of Yahoo! option. You might simply be looking in the wrong category. Within seconds you should receive a list of matching sites.

But directories are not the most extensive databases on the Web, and there is always the chance you will not find what you are looking for. Once you have exhausted all the possibilities at *Yahoo!*, you can scroll down to the bottom of the page and click on a button to go directly on to a **search engine**, such as *AltaVista*, which is more powerful.

Search engines: robots on patrol

Search engines differ greatly from the directories described above. They are immense collections of data, compiled by automated **searchbot** programs 24 hours a day. These robots, or spiders as they are often called, are software programs that scan through millions of web sites and other sectors of the Net to formulate their listings. The spider returns with the mass of data it has found, which is emptied into an ever-expanding database, and the information is then extracted and classified according to keywords. The enormous amount of information they scan makes search engines fantastic tools for detailed research.

Each search engine maintains a unique index, and operates in a particular manner. Different search engines use different robots, scan different pages for different information, use different classification and search strategies and display results in different ways. Before using an unfamiliar search engine for the first time it is always sensible to browse through its help file to get a few tips on what it offers. Most of them attempt – at least nominally – to incorporate the more user-friendly directory style in some way, but trying to keep up with them is a continual learning process.

How do search engines differ?

Here is a quick assessment of a few of the top search sites, in no particular order, adapted from the archives of various online review and statistics sites – for while the help files of the search engines themselves are invaluable, their marketing claims need to be read with a healthy dose of scepticism. (One way to evaluate the different search engines is to read the reviews at the *Search Engine Watch* site.)

- **AltaVista**: The popular *AltaVista* search engine was designed by Digital Equipment Corporation to show off the speed of its system. It is one of the most powerful and most comprehensive search engines online, indexing between 80 and 140 million different web pages and Usenet newsgroups. Its spider, Scooter, searches through all text and coding on the web sites it visits, scouring not only the top page but delving deeper into the site to uncover more detailed information. Then it revisits the site about once a month to update its listings, averaging roughly 6 million web pages and newsgroups a day.

- **HotBot**: Part of the collection of search tools offered by *Wired* magazine, this has been ranked among the most popular search engines. Because it is not yet overcrowded, *HotBot* can be very fast, and is powered by a spider that has indexed some 110 million web pages – competing with *AltaVista* to be the largest database. Although some users question its unusual colour scheme, this search engine includes some unique options; such as using the modal verbs 'should' and 'must' in parallel to filter the results.

You can also elect to search for certain media types or domain names, and you can control the depth of the search by specifying the number of levels to examine in each site.

- **Lycos**: Run by Carnegie Mellon University in the United States, this has been one of the most effective search engines on the Internet. It covers at least 30 million pages, mainly those that have been directly submitted. In addition *Lycos* indexes **FTP** and **gopher** addresses, and features categories for finding pictures, sounds, roadmaps and people. Because of a unique automated feature of *Lycos*, when you access it you will be obliged to visit the version of *Lycos* that is local to the country or region where you are. If this is not an English language version, links to English-speaking versions can be found at the bottom of the opening page.

- **Infoseek**: With a database similar in size to *Lycos*, this search engine **crawls** for sites and accepts submissions for review. Human editors also review many of the pages brought back by the indexing robots. So information can be accessed through channels, similar to categories in a directory, with world news, an e-mail directory and yellow pages. Their listings include searches of the Web, gopher, FTP and Usenet newsgroups. While this is neither the most complete nor the most up-to-date database on offer, its unique approach makes *Infoseek* number six in the rankings of most popular sites, and an effective search tool.

- **Excite**: This search engine has extremely up-to-the-minute listings, although even with around 50 million pages indexed it is not the most exhaustive database available. *Excite* employs a concept-based search mechanism, not just keywords, which returns synonym matches as well. To turn this mechanism off and narrow your search parameters you must use **Boolean** symbols (+ -), which are explained on page 45. One of its helper applications which allows you to pinpoint similar sites can be invaluable when refining a search. *Excite* is also collaborating in several sites on the regional level and provides city guides, a reference section, channels and reviews of other sites.

There are thousands more search tools online, each with a specific user group in mind. Two of them are of special interest to educators: *Education World*, with a database of over 50,000 sites indexed by school year; and *StudyWeb*, indexing 70,000 sites for academics and research. Another handy tool is *Beaucoup*, a directory of roughly 1200 search tools divided into clear topic areas, which is effective for locating that one search engine specially suited to your task. The address for this site, as well as the many sites mentioned above can be found in Appendix D (see pages 111–112). We are now going to take a closer look at one of the search engines, *AltaVista*, to see how it works.

How to use a search engine

You use a search engine by typing keywords into the search box, just like in a directory (see page 39). But because these databases are so large, they have an awful habit of returning far more information than you could possibly sift through in several lifetimes. The information supplied can also be duplicated, out-of-date or irrelevant. (Experts claim that only about 10 per cent of results returned by a search engine will ever be fully relevant.) If you are faced with millions of addresses, as shown in the *AltaVista* search results on the next page, even that small percentage is excessive.

There are several solutions to this information overload. The first step is to choose the section of the Internet you want to search. In *AltaVista* there is a simple drop-down box to select either the Web or Usenet newsgroups.

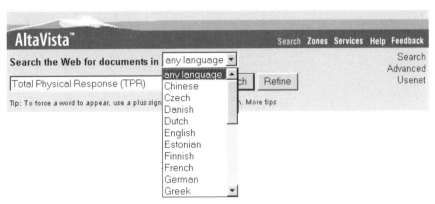

AltaVista's *opening screen, with its drop-down box*

Then you will need to restrict the language of the materials. In this case it would probably be English, although *AltaVista* provides a choice of 25 languages, and a very crude translation application just in case you do find something irresistible in another language.

Because a search engine uses keywords to sort the information in its database, it is essential to have at least a rudimentary understanding of how it sees these keywords, and adapt your search accordingly. Many search engines, in their default setting, look for every occurrence of each keyword, individually and in every possible combination. Looking at the bottom of the *AltaVista* results on the next page you will notice a figure after each word. This is the number of times this word was found.

A search engine usually gives precedence to the first word on the left, as if it were reading a book. This means that it will rate results that contain the first word higher than any of the others, and put them first on the list. Most are case sensitive as well. If you want to find a proper name, such as 'The Coffee House', make sure you capitalise the first letter of each word. This will restrict your search to sites which contain this name. Conversely, if you are looking for information about coffee in general you should not capitalise at all. This finds all instances of the word both capitalised and not.

One way of working is to start with one keyword, which will give you a sweeping search that you can progressively tighten by increasing the number of keywords. This is fine if you have plenty of time to spare. Otherwise, you can search for phrases by enclosing the words in double quotation marks, which forces the search engine to return solely those web pages that match the exact phrase, in that precise word order. This **string search** is convenient for finding poetry, literary quotations, song lyrics and proper names.

Sample results from the AltaVista *search engine*

It also reduces the number of results in a search for a topic. For example, when *AltaVista* looked for the words 'total physical response' as separate keywords it found more than 3 million matches. When it looked for the phrase 'total physical response' it found only 8667.

Using a 'string search' to improve results

More complex 'advanced' searches, like the one shown in the screenshot above, allow you to use **Boolean logic**. To put that in layman's terms, by adding a few mathematical symbols between the keywords you can greatly improve your results. The two most useful are:

+ AND: this symbol requires the search engine to return only results that have both the terms, together.
- NOT: this symbol asks that all sites containing the specified word be excluded. Often used with AND.

There are other possibilities, but because they are frequently incompatible it is best to skim through the help files of the search engine you are using to check their particular use. When plus signs were added to the keywords, *AltaVista* brought back only those sites that matched the three words. The results were reduced to a reasonable 560 matches.

You will notice that there is no space between the symbol and the word. This is crucial. An equally valid way to use Boolean logic is by using the words the symbols are meant to represent: Total AND physical AND response.

To further refine an advanced search enter a range of dates into the fields marked From and To as shown below. If this search were limited to a few months, say between March 24 and August 7 of 1998, only 133 matches would be found in the database.

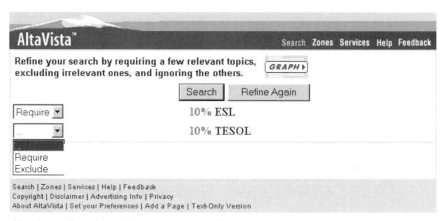

Using Boolean logic and a limited range of dates

One final method to solve the overload problem is hidden behind the Refine button. This gives you a list of topics that the search engine has uncovered during the first search. You decide which ones are relevant, and require or exclude them from the search. This whittles the list down to under a hundred matches, the majority of them relevant to the topic.

Choosing to Require or Exclude terms to refine a search

Natural language search engines: simple questions

How wonderful it would be to ask a search tool a simple question and get a simple response: What time is it in Ulan Bator? What's the weather forecast for Montevideo? What happened on such and such a date in history? Where can I find the lyrics to the Red Hot Chili Peppers' latest release? Actually, *AltaVista* accepts these kinds of questions, though experience has shown that the results are not very impressive. This is where **natural language search engines** come into the picture.

Ask Jeeves is a friendly, real-language search tool. You just ask a question in plain English, and Jeeves responds by interpreting your question in various ways, allowing you to confirm the direction you wish to continue searching. You are given only a few choices, rather than a comprehensive list. And when you click on a question, Jeeves takes you right to the web page where it thinks you will find the answer. Once again, this database is indexed by a live research staff, which means that the search engine is more likely to give you relevant information. It is so easy and fun to navigate that students can use it with little difficulty.

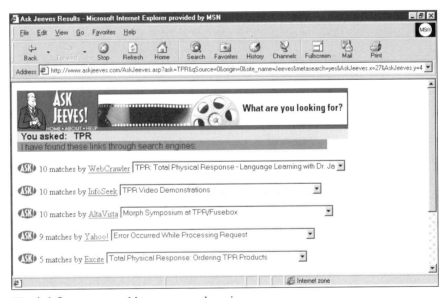

The Ask Jeeves *natural language search engine*

What is a metasearch?

Metasearch tools: collective searches

Ask Jeeves can also be used as a metasearch tool, that is, a search engine that provides simultaneous access to several other search engines, without having any listings of its own. Metasearch tools have evolved from being merely cosmetic improvements – that saved you a bit of time downloading the various start pages of each search engine – to being superb channels to the information stored on the Internet.

ProFusion, Mother Load, Dogpile: the names themselves play on words that seem to imply the best use of this kind of query. With links to so many search engines on a single page you can really unearth a massive amount of material. Clearly, you may have to sift through duplicate listings, but with well-defined keywords this can be an excellent resource for a quick probe of the Net.

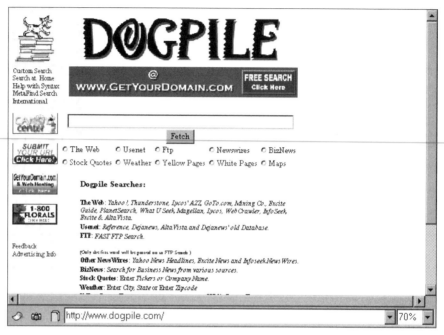

A metasearch tool front page

Searching in the future

The Internet develops quite rapidly, and while all of this is true today, it could easily change tomorrow. No one really knows what will happen, but currently search technology seems to be going towards **desktop search utilities** and **intelligent agents**.

- **Desktop search utilities** are applications that sit on your computer until you are ready to use them. The ones that are currently available let you contact a number of search engines simultaneously, similar to a metasearch tool, but with a bit of customisation. You may be able to specify a number of options: the quantity of sites to visit; the time limit for processing your search; the content required, etc. What makes this type of tool fantastic for teachers is that you can leave it running in the background, and get on with other work on the computer. Once the time has run out, the utility will return with its listing, reporting only those pages which it has personally been able to verify contain the specified information.

- More intuitive **intelligent agents**, which were originally developed for the police and which use neural network technology (a type of artificial intelligence) are now starting to become available to the general public. A review of this technology in *.net* magazine (issue 44, spring 1998) claimed that intelligent agents will offer 'real-time, on-line searches, unattended searches, searches for graphics files, creation of individualised

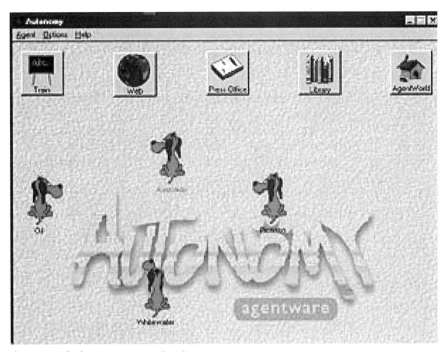

Autonomy's Agentware *search software*

newspapers that can be delivered to your desktop at prescribed times and co-operative search efforts.' For teachers, this means that lesson plans using material from the Internet can then be updated regularly, with almost no intervention on the part of the teacher.

However, artificial intelligence is cutting-edge technology, with quite a steep learning curve, and so not really suited to hurried searches. In spite of this, many teachers will appreciate the educational methodology behind them: learning through personal experience. The tool learns what to do by experiencing searches and then adapting itself to the user's personal needs. Once you have trained your intelligent agent it should be able to adapt itself to your individual search style, think for itself, and allow you to build up an information database of your own.

None of this will be free, however. Unlike the online search engines, which accept advertising to cover costs, desktop utility and intelligent agent developers are commercialising their programs.

Adapting Internet materials

Adapting text-based materials you have found on the Internet is technically quite a simple process really. Whole pages can be saved and then reopened in your word processor, or chosen bits of text can be inserted into a document. All you need to do is a bit of cutting and pasting between your web browser and your word processor. But remember that complying with all applicable copyright laws is your responsibility, as is checking and complying with all legal notices on individual web sites. Where you are in any doubt, seek and obtain the permission of the copyright holder. This applies not only to the downloading of text or images but also to their modification in any way. You can find out more about copyright in the last section of this chapter (see pages 51–53).

To start, when you have checked and cleared all the relevant copyright issues, you will need to open both the Internet application and a new document in your word processor. Then carefully select the area you want to copy.

You can usually highlight text by clicking in front of the first word to copy, and holding your left mouse button down while you drag the cursor to the end of the text. When you release the mouse button, the text should remain highlighted.

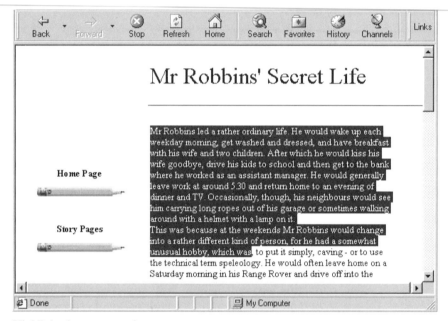

Highlighted text on a web page

The next step is to copy the text as you would normally, and paste the text into the document in your word-processing program. You can now use the features of your word processor to adapt the material to the needs of your class. For example, you may have copied a restaurant menu, but would like to change the prices to pesetas. You may have chosen a song or dialogue to turn into a gap-fill listening exercise. Perhaps you have selected a story that could easily be converted into a jigsaw reading or a movie script you would like to make into an ordering task. But remember to check and clear any copyright limitations first.

Texts can easily be edited and redesigned to be less intimidating as well. Dense paragraphing can be corrected; complex phrases can be simplified. Colours and underlining can be used to focus on certain vocabulary or structures. With a series of modifications the text can be transformed into useful teaching material, without the need to retype the entire document.

Working with images is a bit trickier, but still possible where this is not blocked by any copyright restrictions. You can use pictures and photographs from the Internet, or from other programs and sites, to aid comprehension of texts or make them more attractive, and as prompts for language work. A song could be accompanied by a photo of the band; a news article about a particular event could appear with a map of the area in which it happened; financial reports could include the salient graphs and charts.

Technically, there are two easy ways to capture graphics from the Web. You should be able to click the right mouse button on the selected picture to pop up a menu from your web browser. The menu will be slightly varied, depending on the browser you are using. You may find you can Save the picture as a file on your own computer (as below), or you can choose an option to Copy the picture to the clipboard.

Capturing a graphic from a web page

Then go back to the document you are working on. If you have chosen the Copy option you just need to paste the picture into the document. If you have saved the picture as a file, you will now need to Insert the picture following the instructions in your program help files. Your word-processing package should then allow you to edit the size and position of the pictures from within the document.

Copyright and the Internet

Many teachers are puzzled as to how copyright laws apply to material on the Internet. So here is a general outline of how they do, according to the Berne Convention, an international copyright convention currently adhered to in 96 countries around the world. One note: there is no 'international copyright protection', so authorised use of material will depend on the copyright laws of your country and the rules of your institution (particularly if these are more stringent than the law).

- A work is copyright from the moment it is set down in a fixed form: written, recorded, designed. This includes all digital media such as e-mail and the Web. Under the Berne Convention no notice of copyright protection or registration is needed. Copyright infringement may give rise to criminal proceedings whether the work is housed on the Internet or any other medium.
- The period of copyright protection lasts for the lifetime of the author, to 75 years after his or her death, depending on national copyright laws. Then the work goes into the public domain and may be used without restriction. Information technology is commonly used to compile information from many sources and to write collaboratively. Thus it is frequently difficult to identify the author or copyright holder of Internet material. Copyright of such anonymous works can last for up to 100 years.
- Copyright protection cannot generally be claimed for the following: works that have not yet been set down in a tangible form; short phrases, names or titles; ideas, principles, discoveries or processes; facts and compilations of public information. However, the titles of works can be protected by copyright in certain jurisdictions, for example in France. Furthermore some forms of protection can be afforded to certain of the items listed above; for, example, short phrases (if distinctive enough, like slogans) may be trademarked, discoveries and processes may be patented and compilations of public information can attract copyright protection or protection against unfair extraction in certain jurisdictions.
- The 'Fair Use Doctrine', in some countries called 'Fair Dealing', allows for the reproduction of copyright material for the purposes of scholarship, criticism, quotation, comment, reporting or research. But this is not interpretable as allowing the multiple copying of material for classroom use.

The Fair Use Doctrine is designed to prevent a monopoly on information and to promote research. It is sometimes overlooked however, because it is a complex doctrine with strict limitations that requires a case-by-case analysis. Here is an outline of the limitations of the doctrine:

1 Fair Use is limited by the purpose and character of the use, including whether for commercial use or non-profit educational purposes.
2 It is limited by the nature of the work itself. For example, it would be difficult to defend the photocopying of an entire coursebook under fair use, because coursebooks are intended for use in the classroom.
3 The amount and substantiality of the material copied is limited in proportion to the work as a whole. While no amount is specified, a general rule of thumb is to use no more than 5 per cent of the work, bearing in mind that in the case of a poem copying even one line might be 'substantial' and therefore 'unfair'.
4 Fair Use is also limited by the effect of such use on the potential market for or value of the copyright work. By republishing a work over the Internet you could seriously devalue a copyright owner's work.

As Internet material is usually accompanied by an e-mail address, the best thing to do is to contact the author and ask for permission to use it. You should also follow the guidelines provided by some web sites on the legality of downloading (and reusing) their material.

When copying works which you have gained permission to use with students, the author and publisher must be cited, as well as the title of the work and the date it was published. (Current proposals for proper citation suggest including the e-mail address as author and the subject line as title.) You might then copy a film review to accompany classroom viewing of the same film, reproduce a text to analyse writing styles and structures, copy literary quotations to critique or review. You may not claim them as your own, or incorporate them into any other work for republishing.

For further information see the publications listed in the further reading section for this chapter, or find a legal advisor versed in local copyright law.

Conclusions

In this chapter we have
- looked at how teachers can find materials designed for English language teaching within the morass that is the Internet.
- discussed the various search tools available. We have compared the advantages and disadvantages of directories, search engines, metasearch and natural language search tools.
- suggested a few tips to improve search results when using the large database search engines.
- asked what lies in store for Internet search capabilities in the future.
- looked at techniques for adapting Internet materials for use in the classroom.
- introduced the basics of copyright laws, and how they affect Internet materials.

Looking ahead

- In the next chapter we will discuss what we mean by an Internet classroom, and think about some of the considerations in setting one up, including layout and equipment.
- We will also take a look at how management of an Internet classroom might differ from that of a traditional one.

4 The Internet as a classroom tool

Now is the Windows of our disk contents made glorious SimEarth by this sun of Zork.
Richard v3.0

- What is an Internet classroom?
- A few thoughts on layout
- Equipment considerations
- A look at access speeds
- Internet classroom management

What is an Internet classroom?

An Internet classroom is like an ordinary classroom apart from one thing: the students can use the Internet to complete activities and tasks. The classroom may have just one computer or it may be filled with the latest multimedia equipment. It may be staffed by a team of computer experts or maintained by a few volunteer teachers. It may alternate between being a classroom and a self-access centre or an Internet cafe for the entire school. But it is crucial that the layout and set-up of the room itself reinforce, rather than dictate, your approach to language teaching.

Starting up an Internet classroom will usually have three distinct phases:

1 **Planning**: budgeting; canvassing staff and students for their opinions; finding a location; sketching out equipment needs and layout; getting bids from different ISPs; deciding on the mode of Internet access; contracting a technical expert who understands the educational needs of the school to help with the second phase.

2 **Set-up**: the physical assembly of the room; the installation and **configuration** of all the necessary hardware and software and subsequent testing and piloting; co-ordinating schedules; initial staff training; introducing students to the technology.

3 **Maintenance**: the reconfiguration and repositioning of equipment as necessary; further staff training and development; reviews of initial decisions based on feedback from teachers and students; updating or upgrading of installations; system maintenance, back-up and repair.

Let's now take a closer look at some of these considerations.

A few thoughts on layout

A fundamental consideration when setting up an Internet classroom is space. As in any classroom, the teacher requires adequate space to move around the class and interact with the learners comfortably. In an Internet classroom the amount of space needed increases in proportion to the number of students working in collaboration around each computer. They will need space for note taking as well as open books, book bags and other personal belongings. An ideal classroom would have additional space away from the computers for group discussion, for mingling or work on other tasks.

Then the arrangement of equipment and tables should not obstruct the teacher's visual contact with members of the class, her access to the board or movement between groups of students.

Developing communicative Internet activities for the classroom becomes problematic if the students are seated at individual stations, in small booths or facing the wall away from the rest of the class, such as in the two classrooms pictured below.

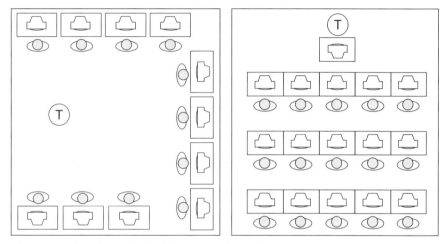

Common designs for traditional language laboratories

Here is one possible layout designed to encourage interaction within a small Internet classroom.

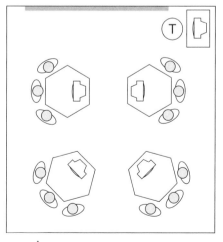

One option for an Internet classroom

Students are placed in small groups so that they are required to negotiate and collaborate on tasks. The teacher can manoeuvre quite easily between the tables in order to respond to learner needs. The students have room to write in their notebooks, and also have a clear view of the computer screen, the teacher and the board.

The positioning of the monitors and other equipment can also help ease communication and sharing between groups of students. By installing the monitors so that they are angled up toward the students from within the table itself, you can improve screen visibility and keep the monitors from obstructing students' line of vision. This also reduces reflected glare from the lights.

Many people see computers as cold and impersonal. It is easy to dispel the perception of coldness by using natural lighting wherever possible, and by concealing cables and non-essential hardware from view. One way to do this is by installing a false floor or raised area under the computers and passing the cables underneath.

In addition, an ideal classroom would offset the wintry frostiness of the equipment by using warm, lively colours throughout. Attractive, relevant posters or visuals – and even a fish tank or a few plants – help create a friendly atmosphere where people enjoy working.

Temperature and dust are obviously factors that need to be taken into account, not only for the comfort of the students, but for the longevity of the computers. Position computers away from direct sources of heat and leave adequate ventilation space behind each computer. Keeping dust to a minimum is a serious concern as this can be one of the leading factors in equipment malfunction, so computers should never be placed directly on the floor where it can be difficult to clean around them. Optimal conditions would include static-free wall-to-wall carpeting in the room to trap dust and improve acoustics, even in locations where carpeting would not customarily be used. Incorporating computers into the desks, as described above, also protects them from dust.

Equipment considerations

Clearly, the feasibility of doing different types of activities in the Internet classroom will depend a great deal on the speed and capacity of the computers you are working with. While it is certainly possible to do basic e-mail activities from just about any computer, to take advantage of all the available multimedia advances that make the Internet so worthwhile for ELT you will need access to fast, powerful computers.

Many of the classroom tasks that are outlined in the next chapter require multimedia computers. This means computers that have the hardware and software necessary to manipulate text, view pictures and play most sound and video files. In addition to the computer, and the Internet connection, it would be useful – though by no means imperative – to have some of the following equipment in an Internet classroom:

- **Printer**: This can be useful for students when adapting material from the Web and can provide them with tangible records of classwork. A printer also makes individualised activities possible: students can print out material suitable for their own needs.

But you may find that having a printer leads to unrestrained printing on the part of students; either because, in their impatience, they click repeatedly on the print icon when their copy does not immediately appear or – as Web documents have no page numbers – they print out very long documents where one page would do. So it is wise to be familiar with your printer's override commands to be able to stop printing at a moment's notice. You might also consider moving the printer out of the classroom to minimise noise and distraction.

- **CD-ROM drive**: it is useful to have at least one of these per classroom. Even if you never use CD-ROMs, this is a convenient tool for installing new or updated software. Most software producers now offer their programs on single CD-ROMs instead of multiple diskettes. A lot of software updates are available over the Internet as well, though downloading software can take a very long time over a slow connection, time during which you may not be able to use the computers for other things.

- **Speakers**: not every computer needs to have speakers, but having at least one set is handy for whole-class listening activities and their correction, as well as for playing background music. Many multimedia computers come with good stand-alone speakers as part of the package. Speakers that are built into the monitor will not be adequate for listening tasks because they do not provide high-quality sound.

- **Headphones**: because students will usually be doing activities in small groups, working at differing speeds and perhaps accessing different materials, speakers are inappropriate for many activities. For that reason it is a good idea to provide each learner with their own set of headphones. Quite reasonably priced headphones are generally fine for most classroom activities; it is only when testing or formally assessing listening skills that you might need the more expensive models.

- **Microphones**: there are three basic types of microphones: ones built into the monitor, ones built into a headset or free-standing ones. Headset microphones leave students' hands free to click and write, and some provide the additional benefit of allowing students to talk to each other – or to the teacher – through the other person's headphones while doing a listening task.

- **Projector**: to give presentations, focus students' attention or give instructions that everyone can see it is sometimes necessary to show one particular program or web page to an entire class. You can do this using simple portable LCD (liquid crystal display) projectors that can be placed on top of a traditional overhead projector, or higher quality projectors that require permanent installation.

- **Scanner**: this is essential for adding students' own photos, illustrations and graphs to e-mail projects, class web pages and student presentations. Scanners come in a variety of models – from small hand-held ones to multi-page desktop versions – priced according to the image quality they render (this is defined as pixel density).

- **Digital camera**: another way to add photos to class projects is by using a digital camera. Instead of using film, digital cameras capture the image on diskette. Each diskette can hold several photos that can then be viewed immediately, incorporated into Internet documents, printed out or manipulated in a graphics program.
- **Video camera**: the most popular – and economical – digital video camera is called a QuickCam. These small, spherical cameras mount right onto the top of your monitor and feed the image directly into your computer. They are frequently used in educational videoconferencing projects that do not require a flawless image. They are adequate for interaction, although the speech is often out of sync with the video image, which is a definite drawback for language teaching. The majority of digital video cameras are still exorbitantly priced, but they may be unnecessary anyway since newer computers often come with software that enables you to digitalise video from a conventional video camera.

One final point to consider when making an investment in computers is the speed at which they become obsolete. There is no need to buy the most costly computers on the market, though it is a good idea to get the best that you can realistically afford. Second-hand equipment may seem like a bargain, but could be outdated before you even get it installed. Try creative funding before settling for equipment that may not be useful for very long.

A look at access speeds

The speed at which you access the Internet will contribute to the success of different types of classroom activities and the amount of preparation they require. Speed will be determined by several factors: the capacity of your computers, the **bandwidth** of your Internet Service Provider and the type of connection you have.

- **Slow access**: while this is fine for basic e-mail and for personal use, most **modem** connections through regular telephone lines provide access that is inadequate for classroom use: downloading sounds, videos or even simple images may be too slow. Modem connections also require a reliable telecommunications infrastructure that is just not always available.
- **Medium-speed access**: this is primarily provided through **ISDN** lines, which are digital telephone lines that make translation from the computer's digital system to the telephone's analogue system unnecessary. This eliminates the lull between the moment you click and actual connection. You lease these lines from your local telephone company, who install and maintain them. However, some ISPs do not cater for this type of access. Where available, this is a moderately priced solution, and generally doubles your access speed. It is sufficient for most class activities, including many listening tasks and activities that involve using abundant visual material. But scheduling is still going to be a deciding factor when planning Internet-based activities, as even ISDN access slows down a bit during peak times of the day.
- **Fast access**: ideally, Internet classrooms would have fast permanent connections through a special dedicated telephone line, a T1. Universities

connected through a T1 line report access speeds up to twenty times as fast as with modem connections. And while this option requires a hefty initial investment, it significantly lowers costs in the long run. Speedy access cuts down on telephone bills, teacher preparation time and precious class time wasted waiting for web pages to load and files to download. It also allows for more flexibility during the lesson and an increased personalisation of tasks according to students' interests once the lesson has started. **Real-time** communication through **videoconferencing**, **telephony** and **chat** becomes positively rewarding at this level.

The Internet continues to advance at an astonishing rate, and information technology advances along with it. Already there has been progress in developing alternative modes of providing high-speed access inexpensively using satellite dishes, cable television and basic electric wiring – through technologies already in place rather than new ones. The satellite reception option is already available in some locations, taking advantage of the digital television satellites in orbit around the globe.

This may finally bring fast Internet access at a reasonable cost to those places where it is now impossible. Certainly, as prices continue to drop and technology continues to improve, the potential of the Internet as a tool for English language teaching continues to grow.

Internet classroom management

All teachers, from the most traditional to the most innovative, can find uses for the Net in their teaching. There is plenty of opportunity for short, quick practice activities as well as full-blown tasks and extensive projects. Though the Internet will not substitute for a good teacher any more than an OHP or a video can, it will immensely enrich your classroom resources and can be used whatever your approach to language teaching.

However, by its very nature as a tool for communication, it does lend itself particularly to communicative and task-based learning. And it is inevitable, really, that your role in the classroom will alter slightly when working with computers. You may feel uncomfortable in this new role at first: you will be teacher, facilitator and Internet guide. Naturally, using the Net as a class-room tool intensifies the need for skilful classroom management and poses new challenges: challenges to facilitating interaction, to time management and to planning. We have touched upon a few of these issues already as they relate to classroom layout and equipment.

In addition, some teachers report finding themselves wanting to take a more authoritative role, in order to counter what they saw as a focus of attention other than themselves and to prevent learners from straying hopelessly off task. This can be the result of a teacher's lack of confidence in her own computer skills, with students – especially younger ones – being quite knowledgeable about the technology. Other teachers report quite a different experience in the Internet classroom, however. They have felt unable to cope with the students' heavy dependence on them for technical guidance.

In both these cases not enough emphasis was placed on practical training in basic computer skills prior to the first lesson – training for both the teacher and the students. Knowing how to switch between windows, hold a mouse comfortably, stop printing or get out of a program opened by accident, for example, will be just as indispensable in the classroom as having the right equipment. And they are amazingly simple procedures to learn in a short time with guidance. When both teachers and students feel comfortable with the technology, less time can be spent on discovering how the tool works and more attention can then be focused on experimenting and taking risks with the language.

- **Teacher training**: despite the ease of **point-and-click** technology, teachers should ideally plan to spend at least a term using the technology for themselves – both as a resource for materials and a teacher development tool – before trying to use it with a classroom full of students. Initial training should usually include a hands-on introduction to all the relevant applications as well as advice on troubleshooting. By the end of the training you should be familiar with the quirks of your particular system, and have uncovered some of the potential obstacles and learned how to solve them or get around them quickly.

  This helps you become more knowledgeable about the content of the Internet as well. The more you explore yourself, the easier it is to know where students have gone wrong, and so save precious classroom time. Do not be afraid to pool your knowledge with other teachers, sharing successful and not-so-successful experiences and lesson plans. If possible, observe other teachers using the Internet, or even team-teach with a more experienced teacher or lab assistant until you feel fully confident. And later, on the occasions when there is a change in the software or hardware in the classroom, you will need to take just a short time to familiarise yourself with it before using it with students, just as you would with any other equipment.

- **Learner training**: More and more students are experienced users of the Internet, and make excellent resources for the less experienced teacher. For the most part such students are delighted to have special knowledge to share, and it is clearly more productive to take advantage of their skills than to worry about them.

  Certain students, however, face computers with intense anxiety, sometimes to the point of technophobia. This does not make using the technology unworkable, but does require very skilful handling. To make Internet classroom activities an enjoyable and empowering experience for them, affective support is essential. Start with non-threatening introductory tasks which build up their confidence in using the technology as well as the language (see page 64 for a sample task). If you can, pair these learners with more confident students during this initial period of adjustment. This allows them to become accustomed to the technology at their own pace.

  Student learning styles and modalities will also colour their approach to using computers in class. For example, students who are primarily kinaesthetic learners might seem to pay no attention while you give instructions, clicking on icons and leaping headlong onto the Web before they really know what to do. They will interrupt and ask a question as soon as they get stuck. They can be impatient or even uninterested in activities that do not allow them to physically control the keyboard or the mouse, and at times will dominate the computer so that other students never get a turn. Predominantly visual learners may panic if they cannot see a demonstration of the activity first or have a diagram outlining the procedure, while strongly auditory learners are usually perfectly content to listen to all the steps before going ahead with the task, even though they may not be looking at you while you speak. You will need to be especially mindful of these preferences when designing tasks, giving instructions and forming workgroups.

A final consideration of Internet classroom management is timing. This can affect you in two ways. Firstly, you will often need some time in the room to physically set up the activity before the lesson. As tight scheduling can make this impossible, you will have to do it once the lesson has started. Move students away from the computers with a pre-task activity that does not require much teacher intervention. Secondly, tasks themselves may take longer to complete – not only because of the occasional delay or technical problem – but also because students become so engrossed in the task that it is hard to persuade them that time is up. Allow for this extra time in your lesson plan.

Conclusions

In this chapter we have
- clarified the term 'Internet classroom' and discussed the different phases involved in creating one.
- looked at a sample classroom layout and the factors to consider in designing a layout for collaborative learning.
- discussed ideas for creating a pleasant working environment for students, to counter any high-tech feel that can be off-putting.
- given advice on equipment for the classroom.
- talked about the ramifications of different access speeds on classroom use of the Internet.
- described how some teachers have experienced a change of role in the Internet classroom.
- suggested basic training needs and how much practice teachers should have before bringing students into the Internet classroom.
- considered how students may vary in their Internet experience and learning styles.

Looking ahead

- In the next chapter we will look at a variety of activities to use in the Internet classroom, and discuss the process of designing them.

5 Internet-based activities

The best attitude is to consider the Web a dancing bear. The mere fact of its existence is remarkable; whether it waltzes is beside the point.
Denise Caruso

- **What makes a good Internet-based activity?**
- **Introducing the Internet**
- **Focusing on language**
- **Reading**
- **Speaking**
- **Writing**
- **Listening**

What makes a good Internet-based activity?

Before you design an Internet-based activity you really need to decide on your objectives. Ask yourself the following questions:

- What are you hoping students will get out of the activity?
- Why do you want to do this activity on the Internet rather than through other media?
- How long do you expect the activity to last: part of a lesson, several lessons, all year?
- Who are your students going to communicate with: each other, another class in the same school, another school in the same city, students in another country, a native speaker, a company or another organisation?
- Are you planning on using this activity with more than one class and/or level?

One point of departure for creating tasks is to look through your course book, pinpointing activities that did not seem to work well with your class, that did not challenge them or engage their interest for whatever reason. Analysing the shortcomings of these activities will frequently suggest an area of the Internet to use for your task: letters that go nowhere hint at e-mail; out-of-date newspaper articles imply use of the Web, as do discussions of films never seen; debating or defending commonly held opinions craves a synchronous multicultural medium such as **chat** or **discussion boards**. There is no one correct tool for every activity or every group of students, so you will need to experiment.

Once you have determined the specific application or applications you would like to use for the activity, the next step is to find the particular area or site you will use: a specific chat room, mailing list or web site for example. You will need to develop specific criteria for evaluating and choosing sites. Though these may vary depending on your situation and the application chosen, useful criteria might include an assessment of instructional elements such as content accessibility, intelligibility and relevance to objectives, as well as functional and design elements such as speed and flexibility, interactivity and user-friendliness.

Having chosen an area or site, it is then a matter of designing an activity that suits both your objectives and the area or site you have selected. Remember that there is no sense in doing activities that are equally well done offline with paper and pen, using the Internet for the sheer novelty factor. Misuse of the tool in this way can be as demotivating for you as for the students. The real benefit for students begins when activities exercise different kinds of learning styles also known as 'multiple intelligences' (see multiple intelligences in Appendix E on page 117), provide a real audience for communication and allow for interaction on both a local and/or international scale. In this way they can enable students to: evaluate, review, publish, compare, negotiate, simulate, create, investigate, hypothesise, organise, bargain, debate, interview, listen, watch, retell, examine, experiment, play, survey and report.

The following sample activities will hopefully give a taste of what is possible. They are divided into six categories (though these categories often overlap): introducing the Internet, focusing on language, and the four skills. While they are designed for use in the small room of networked computers illustrated in the previous chapter, with a stable, medium-speed connection to the Internet, they could easily be adapted for use with larger classes or slower access.

Introducing the Internet

As mentioned in Chapter 4, providing a non-threatening introduction to the technology in the classroom will reduce students' anxiety and can forestall future difficulties. To this end, you might send students on a walking tour of the room, looking at materials you have printed out from the Web and other students' work on the noticeboards, identifying the equipment from labelled pictures, gathering information about how different members of the class have already used the Internet, brainstorming vocabulary they might already know and negotiating groups for the lesson.

Once groups settle around the computers there are many possible activities. You could give them a handout similar to the one below, which moves from identifying their computer, to working with the **local area network** (LAN), using the web browser and its home page, doing a simple search and finally on to simple online communication. A projector is useful to demonstrate each step as the students work through the activity. At this stage it is important that you disregard the quite normal urge to physically assist students unless it is absolutely unavoidable.

Example activity 1: getting to know the Internet

Focus: familiarisation with the tools, vocabulary and navigation of the Net
Session: 3 hours with intermediate level adults

Speaking: discussing options, decision making, chatting
Reading: skimming and scanning for information
Listening: following precise instructions, recognition of new terms
Writing: short personal notes, welcome, graffiti, fan letter, love poem

---

A Quick Tour of the Internet

1. Look at your *screen* and find the name of your computer _____

2. *Double Click* on the *icon* marked **Network**. What are the other computers called?

   _____

3. How can you send a message to the students at one of the computers? Send a welcome message to another group. Copy your message here:

---

4. Internet Vocabulary. Choose ten new words from the list below:

Home page	Access	Real-time	MOO
URL	FAQ	e-mail	Mailing list
Download	RealAudio	Chat	Discussion board
Newsgroup	Bookmark	Link	http
Password	Virtual	Browser	

Now *double click* on the **WWW** icon. What happens? _____

Find the Internet glossary or dictionary and look up your new words. Explain them to your partners in your own words.

In your group, try to put the new words into three categories. Compare your categories with another group. Do they agree?

Category 1	Category 2	Category 3

---

5. Click once on the *Search* button near the top of the screen. Where does that take you?

   _____

6. The teacher is going to give you some tips on finding things on the Internet. Take notes here:

7. Find the answers to as many of these questions as you can.
   a) Who is Mother Shipton and where does she live?
   b) What common child's toy has a Scandinavian web page? Did you have this toy?
   c) Where could you get your handwriting analysed? What do you think of this study?
   d) Find out the 'word of the day' or the 'idiom of the week'. Try to use it in a sentence.
   e) Where is the 'cool site of the day'? Why do you think it was chosen for this honour?
   f) What is Project Gutenberg? When did it begin?
   g) What is on at your local cinema? Are there any films in English you want to see?
   h) Where is the *Exploratorium*? Have you ever visited a similar place?
   i) Who wrote the *Global Encyclopedia*? What could you contribute?

   Now share your answers with another group. What was the easiest to find? What was the most difficult?

   (continued on next page)

8. Choose ONE activity from the list below. You will find a *shortcut* on the main screen that will take you directly to each place.

√ It is time for a break at *Dave's ESL cafe*. While you *browse* around and relax, why don't you write some graffiti on the wall? How many different nationalities are present there? Read some of the messages and reply to one.

√ Identify the Mystery cover at iT's *Magazine*. Try out one of the activities in this month's magazine (teach your dog English, update Shakespeare's lines, write a fan letter to …)

√ Chat at *Worlds Chat*, the virtual space station. First click on the icon from the *desktop*. You will be in the gallery of personalities, called avatars. Choose the character you would like to represent you while you are visiting, remember that this is the only view people will have of you so choose carefully. Now you can enter the space station.

:-) Don't forget to move out of the doorway! What number are you? _____
Are any other people from the class there? Introduce yourself to one of the visitors and find out about them. What time of the day is it in their country? Have they visited *Worlds Chat* before? What do they think about it?

So … what are the English words you learned today?

Focusing on language

There are many ways to focus on language with your students, without restricting yourself to sites specifically designed for ELT. Certain sites lend themselves perfectly to these activities. For example, the many dictionaries and lexicons, with their friendly, interactive interfaces, offer students a chance to work on strategies for learning vocabulary.

Example activity 2: recording vocabulary

Imagine that you have been discussing different ways of recording vocabulary in notebooks, and want to give your students a clearer idea of mind-maps. You might take your students to the *Plumb Design Visual Thesaurus*, which allows students to discover vocabulary by clicking on words and exploring a thread of meaning. There is a simple tool for choosing which part of speech to focus on. It engages, even mesmerises, learners as it goes about creating a three-dimensional map of lexical association. To structure the activity, get students to explain the relationship between each pair of words, or to contrast their uses. Give them a goal such as ending at the same word they started with, without going backwards or repeating.

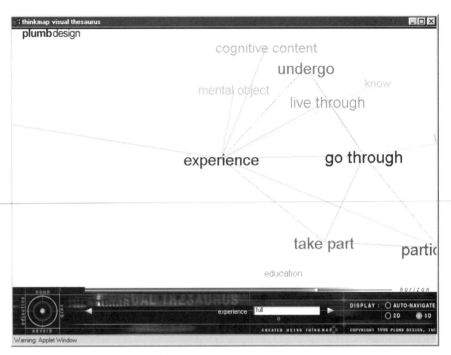

The word 'experience' in Plumb Design's Visual Thesaurus

Example activity 3: reviewing lexis

Another good use of the Internet is as a resource for reviewing specific lexis. This activity is intended to review words used to describe houses. The teacher selects a site or sites that provide students with an insight into other countries and the kind of housing to be found there. At the site students can, for example, visit houses in the country or in the city, in America, Europe or almost anywhere. The houses can range from mobile homes to luxury estates. On page 67 is an example of the kind of site that can be used to provide pictures of different sorts of houses. Underneath it is a chart for students to use while they are studying the site.

Focus: revision of housing lexis
Session: 45–60 minutes with elementary level adults or teens
Speaking: describing photo, responding to feedback
Reading: scanning for information
Listening: critical listening for details, asking for clarification
Writing: reformulating descriptions

In pairs, students complete the chart with information about four houses from the site that they like. You may need to encourage them to take risks, choose houses that push them to use the vocabulary they have just learned. Then they write short descriptions of two of the houses.

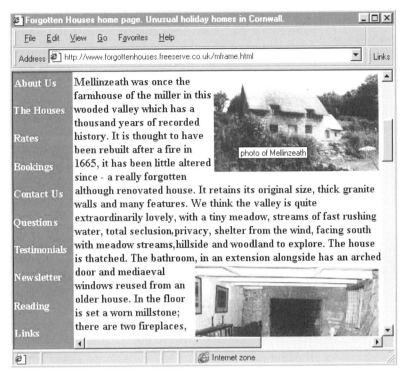

A page from a property rental agent's web site

Let's visit some houses

Your teacher is going to tell you how to open some pages on the Web. Choose different houses and fill in the chart below with the missing information.

	What type?	Where is it?
House 1		
House 2		
House 3		
House 4		

Now choose two of the houses and write short descriptions of them:

I've found a …	We've just moved to a …

(adapted from Adrian Doff and Christopher Jones Language in Use
Pre-intermediate Classroom Book, *unit 8, CUP, 1991)*

The activity can be continued with an information-gap activity by rearranging the pairs. One student reads out a description while the other makes notes on the chart, and then uses the information to find the house being described on the web site.

Example activity 4: a game

Online versions of games and sports are valuable for introducing or reviewing structures such as the imperative, conditionals and the passive voice. These can be played individually, with local teams or – in the full multi-player version – against strangers at a computer in some other part of the world. The inherent motivation of a game is then increased by playing against an unknown native speaker. The students do not have the stress of face-to-face interaction, they have a bit more time to think, and they can stop at any time. The game should be fun, and should also help students notice the differences between the native speaker's English and their own.

Jeopardy, a television game show popular in the United States since the 1960s, also has a multi-player online version. Since the entire premise of this show is to give the contestants an answer and have them formulate the question, it is a site where students can study question formation as homework on their own computer if they have one. But sites like this one do have strict copyright and terms of use restrictions (which you need to check) and do require preparation time filling in the registration form on site.

Example activity 5: giving online advice

The Web can be ideal for looking at particular language structures because many sites are dedicated to one specific category or function. In addition, many of them have personal relevance to the students, which is often missing from textbook activities.

Here is an example of one such activity, involving one of the many online advice columns. This particular site, *Teen Advice Online*, is appropriate for several reasons: the design is clean and fast, the information is updated weekly, the language is formatted in accessible chunks, the site has enormous breadth of scope (teenage volunteers help other teenagers) and of course there is the opportunity for real interaction via chat and discussion boards. It could be inappropriate if students do not relate in any way to the dilemmas discussed on the site.

Focus: introduction/revision of giving advice, language patterns
Session: 90 minutes to 3 hours, with teens, intermediate levels and above
Speaking: discussion of real dilemmas, past or present, and solutions
Reading: reading for detail, skimming and scanning
Writing: defining problems, sharing opinions or asking for advice

Before moving on to the Internet, divide the class into two groups, A and B. Give each group four titles from the advice site archives and explain to students that these are real problems, written by teenagers who want advice. It is important that there is no sharing of information between groups at this time. Here are some examples of titles from this archive:

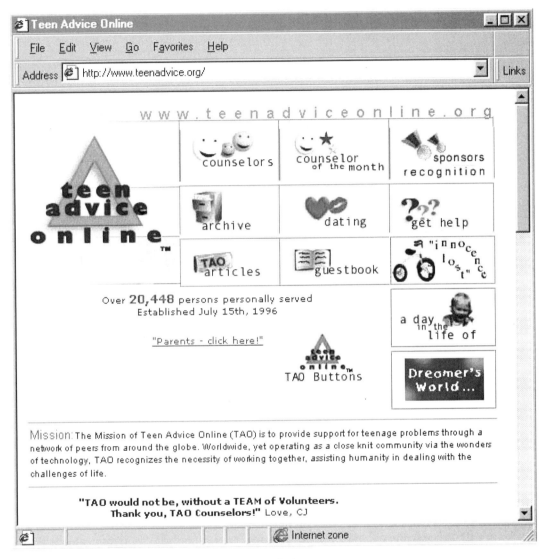

The home page for Teen Advice Online

- *Not the same person anymore*
- *Age gap matters*
- *Getting over him*
- *Mom's new husband*

- *Grounded*
- *They don't call back*
- *Cold feet*
- *Big brother type*

In their groups, or in pairs, students then discuss the titles and guess what the problem is by answering these questions:

Who are the people involved?
What is their relationship?
What exactly is the problem?
What advice would you give this person?

Groups then go online to the archive to check their guesses against the real queries. They search for their titles from the topic index and then scan the text. The focus here is on understanding general meaning.

After students have discussed their reactions to the problems they can reread the text in detail, jotting down the phrases used to ask for and give advice, for example 'what you need to do is …' 'so, the best thing you can do is …' 'you may even want to …' (They will be using this information again during the post-Internet phase of the activity.) Now might be the time to answer any specific vocabulary questions as well. The site usually contains some slang and idiomatic use that is fascinating to teenage learners.

Follow-up activities while you are still online can include: e-mailing in their own problem or advice, using the chat program to share their opinions about the advice given and/or the site, finding out about the organisation or the counsellors.

Finally, once you are offline, pair up students from the two different groups to share information about the problems they looked at, and discuss similar problems they might have had. And of course, focus on the language. Ask students to write the phrases that they discovered up on the board. You could start by comparing the way different languages handle asking for and giving advice. Then you can look at the grammar and talk about collocations, register and frequency of use, as relevant.

This is just one example. There are many versions of this type of activity, based on the multifarious advice and 'how to' sites on the Web.

Reading

You will already have noticed that all of the activities described above incorporate some element of skills work, especially reading. Since the Internet was basically a text medium until a few years ago, reading is still one of the easiest skills to practise on the Net. Many of the classics of world literature vie for an audience with e-zines and cybernovels – magazines and novels that exist only in electronic format – not to mention the flood of paper-based newspapers and magazines published simultaneously on the Web. And with the advent of the Web, reading a computer screen has become a more realistic assignment. Text is well formatted, easy to look at and often broken up by relevant pictures and graphics which aid comprehension.

But texts can be printed out or easily saved and read offline. Why focus specifically on reading in the Internet classroom? Because the text has interactive links, allowing students to read the way the mind often thinks, in a non-linear path. These links can also involve interplay with other readers, the author or the publisher. They can also lead to support materials that are not available off the Internet.

Example activity 6: newspaper headlines

One simple Internet reading activity begins with newspaper headlines. In coursebooks, headline expansion is frequently used as a lead-in to reading newspapers, but because books are a print medium, the headlines and accompanying articles are obviously out of date by the time they reach students. The information gap is in fact artificial, as the headlines are lopped off and placed on a separate page from the texts they belong to.

On the Internet news is constantly updated, so it is always current, and students have a wider range of headlines to choose from. And the information gap is real, since most news services and papers open with a page of headlines divided by topic, each with a link to a summary of the article or the whole article. Further links lead to multimedia support material and background information allowing you to expand the activity in the direction of student interest. The activity below shows how you can exploit a typical news web site. But check first for any copyright restrictions on the site you choose to use.

Focus: lead-in to reading newspapers, review of sentence structure
Session: 30 minutes to 1 hour, with pre-intermediate levels and above
Speaking: talking about current events
Reading: reading for detail, information gap
Writing: expressing opinions

Headlines ...

Visit the Headlines page of a web site, selected by your teacher, for today's top stories. Choose three headlines to rewrite as complete grammatically correct sentences. You might have to guess what the article is about.

1.

2.

3.

Check the article to see if your sentence accurately reflects the headline story. Finally print out one of the articles and read it.

News sites also provide an excellent opportunity to look at cultural diversity: the way different newspapers deal with the same story, or choose the lead story for the front page. Students can easily compare articles from their local newspapers – either the paper edition, or the Internet version if available – with similar stories in the international press. The immediacy of the information provides strong motivation for careful reading, and sometimes sparks a real desire to write a letter to the editor. A link to the editor's e-mail address is usually provided on larger sites.

Example activity 7: an online newspaper

And why not take advantage of the wealth of press material to create a class newspaper? Not *write* a newspaper, but *create* a daily paper that students can read from any computer connected to the Internet: in the classroom, in a cafe, at home, or at work. This becomes an excellent source of discussion topics as the course develops.

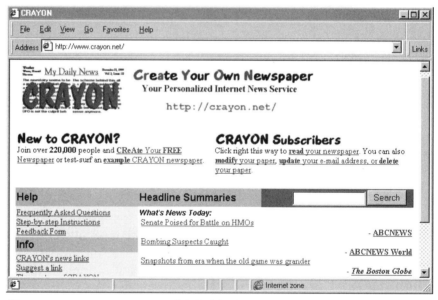

Choose your news sources from the CRAYON *site*

CRAYON – or *Create Your Own Newspaper* – is a special interactive site that allows you to select the content of your own paper from an incredible array of news sources. The majority are newspapers but radio and TV news are well represented. Your class can sample different newspapers and news services as they look at world news, regional news, sports and science reports, comics, etc. Students can choose as many or as few sources as they wish, and put the sections in their preferred order. They make the selections once, and voilà, a paper is born. Your class newspaper will even have a title and motto, which appear at the top of the site every time you open it.

Example activity 8: mystery stories

But the Internet is not limited to the news any more than coursebooks are. There are all sorts of texts, many of which let the reader participate in some way. A common collaborative genre is the mystery. Solving mysteries compels students to pay particular attention to the language – to the time references, and to the verb forms especially. It can be an unobtrusive method of reinforcing vocabulary, since most stories involve a clear setting such as the workplace, the theatre or the home. But once again, why read them online?

Well, it is true, you can find mysteries on the Internet to print out. You can even have short mysteries delivered to your doorstep – or in this case, your e-mail – on a weekly basis by signing up to the mailing list at *TheCase*. But that may be missing the point. When students read mysteries online they can check for extra hints, get immediate feedback on their answer, join in an animated discussion about the story – and maybe even win a T-shirt. At least that is the case at *TheCase* web site.

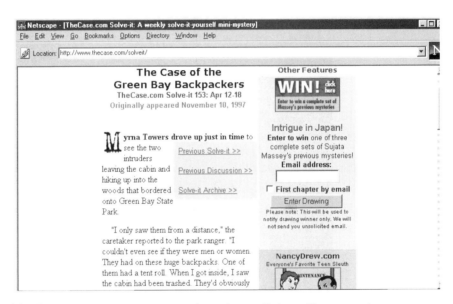

TheCase *site provides weekly mysteries and many links to things mysterious*

Apart from the *Solve-it* short stories, there are many other features including a twenty-part serial. The plot to this weekly serial unfolds according to a story line suggested by the readers. After reading the week's two-minute episode you vote for one of the plot options. Votes are tallied and the writers produce the next episode. At the end of the twenty weeks, a new story begins, so you can join at any time of year. Even though the web site is not designed for ELT it provides ample lesson plans for using mysteries in the classroom and has a parallel site written especially for kids which is also good for use with students at lower levels.

Speaking   As with reading, speaking has been incorporated into the activities above. In fact, it would be almost impossible to keep students from talking as they negotiate their next step around the Internet, whether they are browsing the Web, deciding what to say in a Chat or replying to e-mail.

The Web can provide a real impetus for discussing topics which the artificiality of the classroom setting sometimes curtails: for example, living on another planet, one's first memory, art. How much more tangible the option of space travel becomes when students can travel around close-ups of the planets in NASA's solar system simulator. And how much more interesting it is to describe your earliest memory when you can contribute it to a database of first memories from people all over the world; or discuss the function of memory with scientists at the San Francisco *Exploratorium* web site.

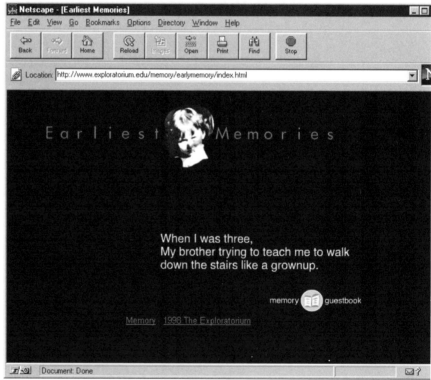

First recollections float past at the Exploratorium *site*

Example activity 9: describing paintings

Art is something that artists and critics having been trying to define for centuries, and yet, in the classroom, the subject is often limited to a few paintings in a coursebook. How can we expect this restricted perspective to be a genuine catalyst for discussion? The following topic-based activity provides learners with exposure to many more works of art within the framework of a structured lesson.

Focus: describing art, joining sentences together
(adapted from Adrian Doff and Christopher Jones 'Language in Use Upper Intermediate' – Classroom Book, unit 3, CUP 1997)
Session: 30 minutes with students from elementary level to FCE
Speaking: describing a picture, negotiating meaning

You can begin with a short reflective discussion on museums: when was the last time they were in a museum? what kind of museum was it? what did they see that they liked or disliked? what style was it? what was the historical period of the exhibit? Ask them what they expect to be in a museum on the Internet.

This leads into a search through artist portfolios at the *WebMuseum* site which students do in small groups. Once the group has found an artist's work that they like, they write out a short description of it – talking about artistic style and mood as well as in more concrete terms. They then read it out to the group at the next computer, who attempt to draw the work as described. Finally, students compare the drawing with the original to see if they were competent in getting their meaning across.

The object of this activity is not to judge the artistic talents of the students, but to work on communicative competence, and it can alleviate any anxiety on the learners' part to stress that. Since the coursebook focuses on joining the sentences together, you could emphasise that aspect of the descriptions through the writing task. More advanced groups, or students who are happy just to speak, can omit the writing, or attempt to write the description as homework.

Still, the real motivating factor in using the Internet for speaking practice has to be its potential for communication beyond the classroom walls through the use of videoconferencing and telephony. Arranging debates and presentations with a class 5000 miles away, with different perspectives on an issue, pushes students to express themselves coherently, examine their rhetoric and work on social strategies. And the tools promote collaboration between schools and experts for investigation and research on cross-curricular projects. If this option is available in your classroom, then you may want to read through other schools' experiences at *The Global Schoolhouse* and skim the ongoing *CU-SeeMe* project site listed in Appendix D (on pages 111 and 110 respectively).

Writing   Example activity 10: keypals

Besides its obvious use as a resource for any writing assignment, the first writing activity that comes to mind for most teachers involves penpals – or keypals, as e-mail penpals are often called. They are an obvious improvement on traditional penpals because of the speed and ease of e-mail. This kind of correspondence transcends many coursebook activities by giving students a real audience for their writing. But it also involves some problems that need to be addressed:

• **Finding partners**: most e-mail projects are instigated and set up by the teachers. Partners are found either by students adding messages to a keypal database or teachers searching the many EFL sites for requests for appropriate partners.

- **Logistics**: messages can be written in class or as homework before going online, giving time for teacher input as needed. Entering the message should take about ten minutes per student or group, but this varies according to the level and the length of the message. Students may have individual or class e-mail accounts, or replies might be vetted through the teacher's e-mail and printed out for students to take away with them.
- **Response time**: because e-mail is such a fast medium of communication students expect immediate replies. When they have not received a letter within a week they are disappointed; after a couple of weeks they can feel completely discouraged. Remind them that perhaps a teacher is ill or students at the other end have different schedules and holidays.
- **Content**: correspondence slackens once students get beyond the introduction stage if they have nothing real to say to one another. Some students may receive cursory replies – or no replies at all.

On the whole, keypal projects rate very highly in terms of motivation and real communication if they are managed properly. Many of the difficulties can be avoided by adequate planning: for example, having more than one keypal or class corresponding at any given time, working in collaboration on projects or long-term tasks and detailing a fairly strict schedule to adhere to.

Example activity 11: greetings, inquiries

But of course, not everyone will be interested in having keypals, and perhaps the first writing activity ought to be more basic. This could be a natural extension of the task they are working on: filling in forms, giving an

Advance notice of a new Quest on the Classroom Connect *web site*

opinion, requesting information. It could be written outside class if students have access to the Net: sending virtual postcards to classmates when away on vacation, or virtual greeting cards for the holidays, or even writing in to explain why they were not in class and get class notes. It might be a task that evolves from the interest students express in current events. For example, over the course of the Mars landing in 1997 NASA provided experts to answer some classes' questions by e-mail. In a similar way *Classroom Connect* has a Quest web site (listed on page 113) which everyone can e-mail (including students as part of a writing task) asking questions and offering suggestions to an expedition team on a Quest in some new part of the world.

Example activity 12: an ongoing project

Once students are familiar with the Web, having browsed around and visited lots of sites, they might like to join an ongoing project. There are all kinds of co-operative writing projects happening all the time, many of them listed on the *Volterre* site with names and contact information (see page 111).

Example activity 13: a web page

Students may also want to publish a class web page of their own. Writing a basic web page is incredibly simple, requiring nothing more than an idea, a word processor and some Web space. In fact, it need be no more complicated than the basic coding we looked at in Chapter 1 (see page 10). There is no need for fancy programming bells and whistles, though some of your students might already be experts, and can take charge of the mechanics of the site. In any case, tutorials on coding web pages are freely available all over the Web – starting with your browser's home page. We include a short list of these sites in Appendix D (see page 114).

Listening   The multimedia content available on the Web is stunning. There is anything and everything from live concerts and interviews to time-honoured radio serials. Your local radio stations may even be available over the Web. Of course, most of the commercial news agencies offer up-to-the-minute reports online. The BBC integrate their web sites with their satellite television and radio broadcasts to provide the fullest resources, and offer worksheets and comprehension activities to accompany them. But it is important to check with these kinds of sites that your proposed use does not conflict with their copyright restrictions. If you are in any doubt, remember to seek and obtain permission.

There are basically two types of video and audio files on the Net:

- Some files or clips require you to click on the file name, and then wait for it to download to your machine before you can play it back. This includes files whose names end in extensions like: .qt or .mov; .avi; .wav. Downloading these files can sometimes take several minutes over a medium-speed connection, but then they can be saved to a file and listened to several times.
- Other clips play back immediately, over a live connection. The most

BBC Radio on the Internet

popular types require a special helper application called the *RealPlayer*™, which plays *RealAudio*™ and *RealVideo*™ files with extensions such as .ra or .ram. You must have a fast, stable connection in order to really enjoy quality sound, since files cannot be saved and listened to offline. But this technology makes live video a reality.

(See Appendix D for sites which give detailed information about these kinds of files.)

Doing Internet-based listening activities requires having a **sound card** in the computer and access to headphones or speakers. It also involves downloading files and installing the right browser helper applications, called **plug-ins**. A multimedia computer has a sound card and also the applications to play back most sound and video files. They come up automatically when you click on the file name. Browsers also come with the latest helper applications already installed. If you come across one that is not included, a link or help window will usually appear asking you if you want to install that particular plug-in. The only costs are usually the connection time needed to download the application. Just follow the step-by-step instructions from the download site and usually the installation process is almost automatic. But it does sometimes take a long time, and slows your connection down, so is not convenient to do during class time.

The control buttons on a multimedia application look quite similar to those on a traditional stereo or video machine: volume, fast forward, reverse, pause. These are familiar to students and so require little explanation.

Students can access unlimited, up-to-date materials to do any activities that are normally possible with an ordinary video or cassette player, and can work at their own pace. When they hear the answer to a question they can immediately pause the playback and write it down. When they have doubts, they can stop the file and listen again. They can play a section over and over without causing the rest of the class to become impatient.

Here are two listening activities based around the topic of films. Films and cinema are regular course book topics which can be very unmotivating for students who have not seen the films. These two activities are designed to get around that problem: the first activity can be done completely offline; the second uses a mixture of downloaded trailers and online *RealAudio*™ along with a web site. With activities like these it is essential to check the copyright hyperlink on the site, often called legal terms of use, and where necessary to seek and obtain the permission of the copyright holder for the planned activity.

Example activity 14: Films: Part one

Focus: describing music, matching themes to films
Session: 30–45 minutes with mid-intermediate and above students
Preparation: select the web site from which you wish to download audio files of a variety of theme tunes from five different films. Check for copyright restrictions and seek permission if necessary. If this is successfully resolved, download the audio files. There can be more than one audio file per film. Place them in a folder on the computer desktop. Also download or write synopses of the same films. If you download these, again check for and resolve all copyright restrictions.
Optional: make handouts of the film synopses; pre-teach relevant music vocabulary; download some actual film clips (if you have permission from the site).

As this activity focuses on film music, it does not involve any comprehension of listening texts as such. Instead, it uses theme music as a way of getting students discussing how music relates to imagery and action.

1 Allocate two or three students to each computer. Ask them to (skim) read the short synopses of four of the five films directly from the computer or from the handout. Keep the music and synopsis of the fifth film in reserve for later.

2 You, or one of the students, sit at a computer with stereo speakers. On the screen in front of you will be the folder you have prepared, containing all the audio files. After the students have finished reading, and dealing with new vocabulary, click on one of the audio files at random. This automatically opens the audio player. It takes a second or two to open and then plays one of the music clips.

3 Students then try to guess which film the music clip is from. They must explain their choices in their own words. For example, 'Very 1950s'; 'The song is so sad and melodic'; 'Oh, I can hear the tension building'; 'It has a great dance rhythm'; 'You can hear drums in the background'.

4 At the end of the lesson you tell the students which music clip is from which film and the students vote for the music clip they think best reflects the film synopsis.

5 During step two, you may be able to slip in some mystery clips from one of the films you have selected. After step four, play the music clip from the fifth film. Then the students try to write a short synopsis of the film including genre, year, location and plot, based on the music. This can be done in class, or as homework. When they have shared their versions, you can compare it with the synopsis of the fifth film.

Example activity 15: Films: Part two

Focus: discussing and reviewing films, expressing preferences
Session: 1–2 hours with mid-intermediate and above students
Preparation: Browse through some film web sites and check and obtain copyright permission for the activity. If this is successful, **cache** web pages from the web site, and download video files from the same site. These web pages need to contain information about three film actors and three film actresses and the video files should contain examples of their acting.

Prepare a handout with a ballot of the three actors and actresses and a list of words and phrases to be used in film reviews.

1 Two or three students sit at each computer. On each computer screen will be the folder you have prepared, containing all the video files and the web pages. Give the students the handouts. Students discuss in groups the actors and actresses listed in the handout, sharing information on their films that they've already seen.
2 Students watch one of the film extracts. They make notes on the quality of the acting.
3 Repeat step 2 until the students are familiar with all the films.
4 The final stage is a pyramid discussion in class to reach a consensus on who is the best actor and who the best actress. A pyramid procedure is where students vote individually, then discuss their opinions in pairs and small groups, and finally as a whole class.

Conclusions   In this chapter we have
- looked at the steps for designing Internet-based activities.
- suggested an activity to introduce students to the Internet classroom in a non-threatening way.
- given ideas and sample activities for using the Internet to focus on language and practise the four skills.
- discussed the helper applications needed for video and audio activities, and the two basic video and audio file types available on the Web.

Looking ahead
- In the next chapter we will look at using the Internet in place of a textbook, and examine some of the implications of online tasks.

6 The Internet as a coursebook

A language course is effective in proportion to the breadth of its contact with the student's interests and the depth of its penetration into his/her emotional life.
Earl Stevick, 1971

- **Why use the Internet as a coursebook?**
- **Designing an Internet-based course**
- **A sample course outline**
- **Evaluation and further research**

Why use the Internet as a coursebook?

As we have seen in Chapter 5, you can use the Internet as a basis for activities to accompany your coursebook. You can also go one stage further and use the Internet as the basis for your course; or even as your 'coursebook'. The Net's huge range of material and the methods of communication it offers make it particularly suitable for the following types of courses:

- short, intensive courses that require a wide range of flexible tasks to meet the needs of a constantly changing student population
- advanced-level content-based courses that call for unlimited authentic materials
- EAP courses that demand detailed research and note-taking
- ESP courses that focus on specialised information and lexis
- Business English courses that aim to provide real-life situations and multicultural communication skills for the marketplace
- collaborative project-based courses that need fast, dependable international communications
- after-school courses whose objective is to supply a fun, enjoyable environment for younger learners to practise what they have learned

In short, it is suitable for any course designed around the specific needs of a particular group of students. There is a growing trend toward these specialised courses, and published coursebooks and textbooks cannot cater for the specific needs of particular groups of students. This is where the Internet steps in. Not to replace the classroom, or the teacher – or in fact, any of the other classroom tools that are currently in use – but as a source of material, an instrument for real communication, a supply of internationalism and even a tool for edutainment. An Internet-based course can meet the specific needs of your group of students because the Net gives you a more cost-effective and efficient means to adapt your materials to fit them.

In addition, the Internet has, as we have seen earlier, the advantages of providing up-to-date, authentic material in English, and opportunities for real communication with native and non-native speakers. It can also allow students to discover language for themselves in a more immediate way than by reading a textbook.

That said, replacing your coursebook with the Internet is clearly not appropriate in all situations. You may be working within a set curriculum that does not allow for flexibility, or under time constraints that do not permit you the leeway to develop a separate syllabus for each individual class. The coursebook may be an integral part of your syllabus and assessment scheme. In any case, a transition of this kind requires careful consideration of many factors including, but not limited to:

- the needs and expectations of the students
- the role of the school or faculty within the community
- the syllabus criteria
- the course objectives
- the time realistically available for planning

This last point is crucial, because without the ready-made practice materials of a coursebook you will need to spend quite a lot of time planning, to make sure all the necessary skills and language are practised adequately, and to provide well-graded activities and tasks.

Designing an Internet-based course

Once you have decided to use the Internet for the core material of your course, you will then have to analyse your students' needs, plan your course's content and methodology, research your material, and plan your activities in detail. You will also need to consider how you are going to recycle new language from the Net, how you are going to ask students to record their work, and how you are going to assess this work.

Analysing students' needs: There is certainly no reason to discard a well-developed needs analysis tool that is already in place. You can quite simply adapt your current methods to include questions about students' prior experiences with computers and the Internet, and the role they feel the technology should play in the lessons.

Negotiating the syllabus: Because a course of this type allows you greater freedom to adapt materials according to students' interests, you might want to add an informal questionnaire to your established needs analysis. This would be the first step in negotiating the syllabus by contributing student input to the thematic and situational content of the course. Students would need to return the completed survey to the school early enough to allow you time to compile the results and plan the course.

Planning the course content: After you receive the students' input, you will need to survey the Internet materials currently available to fit the specific topics, situations and activity types they have highlighted. This will help you decide how much of the course should be centred on the Internet, and when you will need to bring in other teaching tools. Then, on the first day of the course, you could present your proposed syllabus to the students as a discussion document.

Another option is to re-examine the syllabus for your existing course, incorporate some of its strengths and notice areas that could be improved by use of Internet-based activities. At this point you will need to decide whether you should keep the same basic focus or whether your students might benefit from a shift of emphasis; for example, toward either a more structure-based syllabus or a task-based syllabus. But whatever format your syllabus takes, you will need to establish realistic linguistic and communicative goals, and make sure that your Internet-based activities and tasks support those goals.

Designing tasks and activities: When your students are going to be working directly on the Internet it is clear that you cannot grade the materials – though you can choose them carefully. Where the text is difficult, the tasks can be simple to ensure their achievability. The process of designing tasks for an Internet-based course will be similar to the one described in Chapter 5, but it is crucial to have a clear set of criteria to help you evaluate potential activities. Here is one, adapted from an extensive task-design checklist:

Good tasks should …
1 have objectives that match the communicative needs of learners.
2 allow for flexible approaches to the task, offering different routes, media, modes of participation, procedures.
3 require input from all learners in terms of knowledge, skills, and participation.
4 allow for different solutions depending on the skills and strategies employed by the learners.
5 involve learners in expressing their attitudes and feelings.
6 be challenging but not threatening, and promote risk-taking.
7 promote learner-training for problem-sensing and problem-solving (i.e. identifying and solving problems).
8 ensure cost-effectiveness and a high return on investment (i.e. the effort to master given aspects of the language should be functionally useful either for communicating beyond the classroom, or in terms of the cognitive and affective development of the learner).

Criteria adapted from: Chris Candlin 1987 *Towards task-based language learning* in Candlin, C. and D. Murphy (eds.) 1987. *Language Learning Tasks*. Englewood Cliffs, NJ: Prentice-Hall.

You can either pre-select the linguistic content of the course at this point, based on your curriculum goals and the specific materials that you are going to use, or later, as you monitor the activities and notice the specific needs of your students.

Students' work: 'Ephemeral' might be the best way to describe electronic writing and communication. This means that one of the side benefits of using the Internet in the classroom is a reduction in the amount of paper produced – the so-called paperless classroom. Reading texts may remain on a remote computer. Exercises can be handled online. Homework and writing exercises may be submitted on diskette or by e-mail. So one of the things that you will need to think about at this point in the design process is how you are going to recycle the new language encountered on the Net and what tangible record the students will take away with them.

A student portfolio might answer these needs, and provide a document for later assessment. It might include various handouts and reports, a reflective log of Internet sessions, notes on vocabulary including new-found collocations, printouts of e-mails sent and received, a diskette with the bookmark file of web pages visited, a·bank of screenshots from sessions, projects such as presentations, designing web pages, a newsletter, etc., together with their notes on the process of working on them. Students can then refer to their individual portfolios and groupwork for vocabulary and structures to focus on during cyclical review sessions.

Assessing learners: The move away from paper, and the fleeting nature of the Internet itself, may bring challenges to the assessment of both individual tasks and overall learning. Tasks can have transient physical substance, as in the use of chat – which, like conversation, is difficult to analyse. Collaborative learning, which is the backbone of communicative Internet-based courses, makes it difficult at times to assess individual contributions to the lesson. But the Internet can also provide you with unique tools for the correction of students' work. For example, writing tasks can follow a natural drafting and reformulation process via e-mail, with you providing links from specific student errors to appropriate grammar references on the Web.

The methods of assessing collaborative learning during Internet-based courses are the same as those for an ordinary course: self-assessment, peer-assessment and group assessment.

- **Self-assessment**: This could include getting students to examine and report on their own cognitive processes when dealing with Internet texts (e.g. Do I skim read before closer reading? Am I noticing the differences between my text and my teacher's reformulation?) and review their short-term goals as appropriate. For a sample self-assessment questionnaire for e-mail writing, see the 'Strategy Inventory' e-mail address (listed on page 113).
- **Peer-assessment**: This can include getting classmates to provide feed-back on both work in progress and completed work. This also gives you insight into how individuals have contributed to a group piece of work.
- **Group assessment**: This is your assessment of the final output of groupwork. Although this does not separate out individual contributions, students themselves will be able to make good use of the feedback.

A sample course outline

Now let's take a quick look at a specific sample course to get a better understanding of how a course like this might develop.

An Advanced Intensive Course

Students: 10–20 young adults, multilingual group
Level: mixed-level advanced (all students post-FCE)
Course: two-week intensive, not geared toward any specific exam
Session: five hours English daily (in class and on excursions)

Intensive Courses: Advanced English

Please complete this questionnaire and return it to us as soon as possible to ensure that your course is tailored to your preferences and interests.

1   Which of these topics would you be really interested in working on in class? Is there a special topic you would like to add?

The Arts	Relationships
Current Events	Schools and Education
Health and Medicine	Travel and Places
Jobs and the Workplace	World Issues

2   Try to define each topic in your own words (for example: What area of the arts interests you? How do you interpret the topic 'travel …'?)

3   Choose two activities that you might like to do within each topic.
    Here are a few ideas to help you decide:

chat with someone in another country	listen to a news programme
watch a film or documentary	read a short story or travelogue
design a web page	discuss options for your next holiday
write a report or give a formal presentation	visit schools in different countries

4   Now tell us a little about any previous experience you have had working with computers, or with the Internet.

For this course you might use an informal questionnaire such as the one outlined above, faxed or mailed to students well before the start of the course. Then you can either select and refine from modules that have already been prepared, or develop a new syllabus and work on activities and support materials.

This course could then be outlined in a modular format. For example, modules for the introduction to the Internet, review and closure might remain fixed in the cycle, while thematic units could be selected to fit learners' preferences compiled from the questionnaire, as shown in the chart below.

Week 1	Day 1	Day 2	Day 3	Day 4	Day 5
	Welcome Introduction to the Net	Topic 1 The media	Topic 2 Travel	Topic 3 Free time	Projects and revision
Week 2	Day 6	Day 7	Day 8	Day 9	Day 10
	Topic 4 Sports	Topic 5 Politics	Topic 6 The environment	Projects and revision	Evaluation and end-of-course excursion

General Advanced English: Intensive Syllabus

- **Day 1: Introduction to using the Internet**
  Task: getting familiar with the computer
  Language focus: vocabulary of the Net and navigation tools
  Skills practice: Read – skim and scan
                     Listen – follow precise instructions
                     Write – short note, graffiti, a fan letter
                     Speak – discuss options, make decisions, chat

- **Day 2: The media – a look at the news**
  Task: building an online newspaper of your own – to take home with you
  Language focus: revision of the past, reporting, newspaper sections
  Skills practice: Read – in-depth style analysis
                     Listen – gist, comprehension of newscast
                     Write – short editorial
                     Speak – express likes/dislikes, compare differences

- **Day 3: Travel – questions and answers**
  Task: making travel arrangements, meeting someone from abroad
  Language focus: asking and answering various questions about travel plans
  Skills practice: Read – for specific information
                     Listen – turn taking, detailed prices/schedules
                     Write – request information, fill in forms
                     Speak – probabilities, problem solving, consensus

- **Day 4: Free time – hobbies and interests**
  Task: preparing presentations about personal interests
  Language focus: habitual present and past, express preferences
  Skills practice: Read – search for relevant information
                     Listen – sound bites from film/TV/music
                     Write – presentation, review, biography
                     Speak – find points in common, plan

- **Day 5: Individual presentations, extension and review session**

- **Day 6: Sports – beyond the Olympics**
  Task: predicting the results of a sporting event
  Language focus: reported speech, futures, conditionals, sports idioms
  Skills practice: Read – understanding rules
                     Listen – 'the Sports Babe' radio Web-cast
                     Write – comments to Web board
                     Speak – discuss possibilities, predict results

- **Day 7: Politics – so you want to buy a president?**
  Task: electing a new representative/president/prime minister
  Language focus: passives, political-speak, debating
  Skills practice: Read – genre analysis, party-platforms
                     Listen – for tone/emotion, factual error
                     Write – formal letter to leader
                     Speak – support opinions, polite informal debate

- **Day 8: The environment – issues and policy**
  Task: Finding alternatives to modern problems, prepare informative web page
  Language focus: Green lexis, giving advice, disagreeing
  Skills practice: Read – diagnose problem, find alternatives
                     Listen – short news clips for gist
                     Write – petition, note of protest
                     Speak – inform, discuss dis/advantages

- **Day 9: Presentations by group, extension and review session**
- **Day 10: Evaluation and assessment – end of course excursion**

Once materials have been chosen and activities designed, you can produce an outline of the course for the students to refer to. Because the outline for this course (see opposite page) is neither exclusively structural nor functional/notional in design it is a friendly starting point – students are encouraged to think about the course in several different ways. Although the language focus of each day may turn out to be quite distinct from the one listed here, this type of syllabus can be reassuring to students who come from a variety of educational backgrounds.

Evaluation and further research

At this point in time, investigation into the effectiveness of Internet-based activities is tentative and the findings incomplete, so any evaluation of the effectiveness of your syllabus is a valuable addition to research in the field – hopefully to be written down and shared with colleagues. Besides the obvious teacher and learner feedback on the course, it might be useful to look at some of the following points:

- the quality of interaction – both online and in the classroom (among groups, between learners and the teacher)
- the suitability of the medium as a source for text
- the effectiveness of the tool as an alternative to traditional listening comprehension
- learner personality types and their preferences between various computerised communication tools
- the strategies used in traditional and Internet classroom tasks
- the role of the teacher in Web-assisted language learning
- discourse analysis of electronic communication and its application to the teaching of writing
- the effects of using the Internet as a coursebook on student assessment and testing

The implications of current research for the use of Internet-based listening seem to be that the computer can be more effective than traditional tools if learners are allowed to listen at their own pace, and if exercises are provided either on-screen or online rather than requiring the students to look down at their notebooks. There have been some interesting studies into the use of multimedia for developing listening skills; see Brett 1996 in this chapter's section of Appendix E (page 118). But clearly, long-term research into the effectiveness of the tool is needed across the board.

Conclusions

In this chapter we have
- looked at the rationale for using the Internet as the basis for specialised English courses.
- discussed the steps involved in designing an Internet-based course, from analysing your students' needs to assessing collaborative learning.
- given a simple outline of an Internet-based course designed for a specific group of advanced-level students attending a two-week intensive course.
- pointed to the lack of relevant research and mentioned some areas that teachers could evaluate.

Task File

Introduction

- The exercises in this section all relate to topics discussed in the chapter to which the exercises refer. Some expect definite answers while others ask only for the reader's opinions.
- Tutors can, of course, decide when (and if) it is appropriate to use the tasks in this section. Readers on their own can work on the tasks at any stage in their reading of the book.
- The material in the Task File can be photocopied for use in limited circumstances. Please see the notice on the back of the title page for the restrictions on photocopying.

Chapter 1
What is the Internet?

A What is the Internet? Pages 1–2

Complete the text about the Internet with these terms, without referring back to Chapter 1. Then check your answers with this section of Chapter 1.

ISP   online   modem   multimedia   telephone lines

> To get on the Internet you need a computer, a telephone line, a
> _____ and an _____.
>
> To access the video, audio and interactive files on the Internet you will need a powerful computer which can handle these _____ components.
>
> You don't need a special telephone line, although obviously if you only have one line you will not be able to make telephone calls at the same time that you are _____.
>
> Most new computers have a built-in _____ , which translates the digital language of the computer into the analogue language used on _____.
>
> You get access to the Internet via an _____.

B Applications and their uses Pages 3–5

Complete the chart.

Use	Application	Text-based and/or multimedia?
You can type messages which other people can read immediately.	chat room	text-based
You can send messages and documents to individuals and organisations.		
You can communicate live by video.		
You can exchange e-mail messages about a particular topic.		
You can view documents that are connected to each other by clickable hypertext links.		
You can discuss a topic with everyone in the same group, but over the Internet, not through e-mail.		

C How to use basic e-mail Pages 6–9

Label this screenshot from an e-mail program.

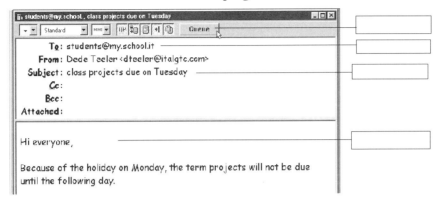

D How to use a web browser Pages 11–13

Which part of this page on *Netscape* would you click on, or point to, if you wanted to:

a   return to your web browser's home page?

b   mark a web site for future use?

c   move down the page?

d   view this month's version of a magazine web site that you visited last month?

e   type in a web site address (URL)?

f   go back to the last page you saw?

Chapter 2
The Internet in teacher development

A The reference library: the World Wide Web   Pages 17–22

1   Number these Web resources 1–10 in order of personal importance to your development as a teacher (1 = most important).

- ☐ professional associations
- ☐ journals and newsletters
- ☐ academic databases
- ☐ distance-learning courses
- ☐ online dictionaries, grammars and encyclopaedias

- ☐ practical classroom ideas
- ☐ publishers' catalogues
- ☐ grants and scholarships
- ☐ information for research
- ☐ job listings

2   Which of these web sites would you like to investigate?

www.puzzlemaker.com	A site where you can make crosswords and other word puzzles quickly and easily
www.iatefl.org	The website of IATEFL
www.pilgrims.co.uk/hlt	The journal *Humanising Language Teaching*, edited by Mario Rinvolucri
www.rpi.edu/dept/cdc/jobsurfer	Job databases
www.richmond.edu/~writing/wweb.html	A handbook for all writers and would-be writers
www.eslcafe.com	*Dave's ESL Cafe*
www.pacificnet.net/~mandel	Teachers' tips and ideas

B The cubbyholes: mailing lists   Pages 23–28

1   Are these statements true or false?

a   You always have to pay to subscribe to a mailing list.
b   Messages from a mailing list do not appear automatically: you need to ask the list to send them.
c   If you send a message to a mailing list, it goes to everyone on the list.
d   You can't send messages to an individual on a mailing list.

Dede Teeler *How to Use the Internet in ELT* © Pearson Education Limited 2000
PHOTOCOPIABLE

2   Which of these options would you use in the situations below?

Digest   Index   Archive   Nomail   Mail   FAQ

a   Before you send off a query to the mailing list you want to check if there is any information about it in the list already.

b   You don't want any messages for the next two weeks.

c   You want a list of today's messages.

d   You want to check if other people have already asked the question that you need an answer to.

e   You want all today's messages sent to you as one message.

f   You don't want to download all the messages – you want to read them in the newsgroup.

g   A week ago you asked for no mail to be sent to you. Now you want to receive messages again.

C   The noticeboard: newsgroups   Pages 28–31

Choose the right answer.

a Newsgroups are:	– discussion groups of current events – discussion groups, organised by subject – discussion groups conducted in real time
b Messages in a newsgroup are organised:	– alphabetically – by subject
c A newsgroup message can be read:	– by everyone on the Internet – only by other members of the newsgroup – only by those to whom you send it
d To join newsgroups you need:	– your own web site – a newsreader program
e Access to different newsgroups is limited by:	– your news server – your newsreader

D   The teachers: chatting and MOOing in cyberspace   Pages 31–35

What are the advantages and disadvantages of these different discussion forums? Complete the grid.

	Advantages	Disadvantages
Mailing lists		
Newsgroups		
Chat programs		
MOOs		

Chapter 3
The Internet as a materials resource

A Why use the Internet for materials?   Page 36

Some issues to consider   Page 37

Complete the chart.

Using material from the Internet	
Advantages	**Disadvantages**

B Expanding your search: using browsers, directories and search engines   Pages 38–47

What is a metasearch?   Pages 47–48

Searching in the future   Pages 48–49

1   Choose the right search tool for each search: a browser, a directory, a search engine, a natural language search engine, a metasearch tool or an intelligent agent.

   a   You want to ask a simple question and get an answer.

   b   You want as many relevant web sites as possible.

   c   You want to be able to access the lists of several search engines simultaneously.

   d   You want a live online search.

   e   You want to find a web site that you know exists, and for which you don't need an extensive search.

   f   You want to look at a category of web sites, rather than one in particular.

2 Look at the screenshot of *Yahoo!* on page 40 and choose two categories that sound interesting. What material might they provide for your students?

3 Which of the search engines listed in the chapter:

a provides local versions of sites, in the local language?

b looks for sites by concept, not just keywords?

c offers you a way of refining your search with the verbs 'should' and 'must'?

d has the most web pages?

e reviews pages brought back by the robots?

4 Think of three questions you would like to ask *AskJeeves*.

a _____

b _____

c _____

C Adapting Internet materials   Pages 49–51

1 What are the steps for:

a copying a text from the Internet onto your word processor?

b inserting an image from the Internet into a document in your word processor?

2 Once you have the text or image in your word processor, what changes might you make?

D Copyright and the Internet   Pages 51–53

Are these statements true or false?

a All material on the Internet is protected by copyright.

b Copyright protection ends with the death of the copyright holder.

c The name of a book is protected by copyright.

d Under the Fair Use Doctrine, you can copy an entire work, provided it is for educational purposes.

e Before you copy and/or adapt anything from the Internet for use in class, you should get the permission of the copyright holder, if at all possible.

Chapter 4
The Internet as a classroom tool

A What is an Internet classroom? Page 54

What is involved at each of the following stages in setting up an Internet room in an institution? Make notes from memory in the chart below. Then check them with the chapter.

Stage	Actions
Planning	
Setting up	
Maintenance	

B A few thoughts on layout Pages 54–56

1 Complete the sentences.

a In an Internet classroom teachers need to be able to

_____

b And students need to be able to

_____

2 Which of these two designs for an Internet classroom is preferable and why?

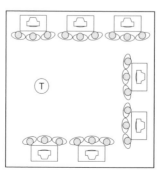 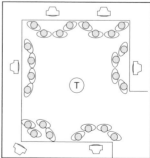

Draw your ideal layout for an Internet classroom suitable for twelve students using four computers. How does it compare with the design shown at the bottom of page 55?

C Equipment considerations   Pages 56–58

Which of these pieces of equipment do you think would be essential in your computer classroom, and which optional? Write E or O next to each.

- ☐ powerful computers
- ☐ printer
- ☐ CD-ROM drive
- ☐ speakers
- ☐ headphones
- ☐ microphones
- ☐ overhead projector
- ☐ scanner
- ☐ digital camera
- ☐ video camera

D A look at access speeds   Pages 58–59

Complete the chart.

	Type of connection	Enables you to ...
Slow		
Medium		
Fast		

E Internet classroom management   Pages 59–61

Which of the following statements do you agree with?

a I plan to spend at least a term using the Internet myself before using it in class.
b I would like to observe other teachers working in the Internet room and then do some team-teaching before I use the Internet in class alone.
c Students' different learning styles are not one of my considerations for planning Internet-based activities.
d I wouldn't like my students to know more than I do about the Internet.
e Internet-based lessons need much more careful time management than other kinds of lessons.
f Most of my students are experienced Internet users.
g I would like to control quite closely what my students do on the Internet.

Chapter 5
Internet-based activities

A **What makes a good Internet-based activity?**   Pages 62–63

1   Number these stages for designing an Internet-based activity in the right order, from 1 to 4.

☐ finding and evaluating a specific application

☐ finding an activity from the coursebook that didn't work well

☐ designing an activity using a specific application

☐ choosing an application that will make the coursebook activity work more successfully

2   Match the application with its most suitable use.

Application	Use
mailing lists	penpal letter exchange
newsgroups	exchanging written opinions about life in outer space
e-mail	virtual meeting with a class in another country
web page(s)	comparing news reports in different newspapers
chat program	exchanging written opinions in real time about current affairs
videoconferencing	receiving regular e-mails discussing football

3   What questions would you ask yourself when choosing a web site or an area of the Internet for a classroom activity? Write them in the chart under the appropriate heading.

Content	Design
Is the material relevant to students' lives?	How user-friendly is it?

B Introducing the Internet   Pages 63–65

Look at the worksheet on pages 64–65. How would you adapt it for use with a group of your students? Would you:
– shorten it?
– divide it into shorter sessions?
– change some of the questions?

C Focusing on language   Pages 65–70

In the grid below write the addresses of these web sites that are useful for focusing on specific language and make notes about each one (in the columns provided).

Website	Address	Language focus	Level	Skills
Plumb Design Visual Thesaurus				
Jeopardy				
Teen Advice Online				

D Reading, Speaking, Writing, Listening   Pages 70–80

1   Complete the chart by ticking the skills that could be practised using each type of material or activity.

Material/activity	Reading	Speaking	Writing	Listening
Designing a class web page				
Webmuseum gallery visit				
Keypals: e-mail exchange				
Finding practical information (e.g. flight details)				
Film clips				
Videoconferencing				
CRAYON				
Following an expedition (e.g. a space mission)				
Radio broadcasts				
TheCase				
Newspaper headlines				

2   Which of the materials and activities above would you like to use? Choose six and put them in order of preference. How would you maximise their interest for students?

Chapter 6
The Internet as a coursebook

A Why use the Internet as a coursebook?   Pages 81–82

What would be the advantages and disadvantages of teaching an Internet-based course to your students?

Advantages	Disadvantages

B Designing an Internet-based course   Pages 82–84

Number these stages for designing an Internet-based course in the right order, from 1 to 10.

- – design tasks and activities for recycling language
- – plan the course outline
- – analyse the students' needs through a questionnaire
- – discuss your proposed course outline with the students
- – consult the students about the course syllabus
- – plan feedback and course evaluation procedures
- – plan procedures for the assessment of student work
- – decide on the course methodology and content
- – design tasks and activities for teaching new language
- – look at what's available on the Internet

2   How would you get students to record their work in these activities from Chapter 5?
   a   Following a thread in *Plumb Design Visual Thesaurus*
   b   Playing an online game such as *Jeopardy*
   c   Giving online advice at *Teen Advice Online*
   d   Reading an online magazine
   e   Finding hotel information from the online *Yellow Pages*
   f   Sending e-mails to friends
   g   Discussing art on the *Webmuseum* site

C A sample course outline   Pages 84–87

A group of upper intermediate students have said in their pre-course questionnaire that they would like to cover the topics in the chart below. What Internet-based tasks could you give students interested in these topics? If you can find relevant sites, add them to the chart.

Topic	Tasks/activities	Relevant sites
current events		
the media		
relationships		
Shakespeare		
travel		
fashion		

D Evaluation and further research   Page 87

Which of these areas of teaching ELT with the Internet might you be interested in investigating (in the course of your teaching)?

Number them 1–8 in order of importance (1 = most important).

☐ *The quality of interaction*
How communicative can the Internet classroom be compared with the traditional classroom?

☐ *The Internet as a source of text*
How effective and appropriate are texts from the Internet for classroom use?

☐ *The Internet as a source of listening materials*
Are listening tasks using the Internet an improvement on the conventional ones?

☐ *Learner styles*
How do different learner personality types benefit from Internet-based tasks?

☐ *Classroom tasks*
Do teaching strategies differ in Internet and traditional classrooms?

☐ *The teacher's role*
How is the teacher's role changed when lessons are based on the Internet?

☐ *Discourse analysis*
Are there differences of register and style in Internet texts that have implications for teaching?

☐ *The Internet as coursebook*
What effect does this have on assessment and testing?

Glossary

access	connection to the Internet
address book	a list of e-mail addresses, stored in your e-mail program
analogue	a form of continuous representation, e.g. a clock whose hands move continuously around the face is an analogue clock. Sound itself exists in an analogue form, and has to be converted to a digital form to be read by a computer. Compare **digital**.
application	a program that performs a specific task, which is controlled by the user, e.g. a word-processing program, or a browser
bandwidth	the capacity of a communication line along which data flows. The higher the bandwidth, the faster the data can move.
Bitnet	an academic network of discussion groups
bookmarks	a list (in Netscape browsers) of web site addresses that you have stored for easy access. When you click on a web site address in this list you go directly to it, without having to type the address in the location box in your browser. (See also **favorites**.)
Boolean logic	a system of logic which uses two values, such as 'true' and 'false'. It is used when typing keywords in a search. Common Boolean functions are AND, OR, NEAR and AND NOT. These words are added to the keywords to refine the search.
browser	a program that allows you to download web pages from the Internet onto your computer. Two of the best-known browsers are Netscape *Navigator* and Microsoft *Internet Explorer*.
cache	to store the web pages you visit in your computer; **cache** is also the name for the part of the hard disk where these pages are stored temporarily
channel	in a chat program, a virtual space where people can write live messages to each other
chat	real-time communication, typing and reading messages, with other people in the same 'chat room'
configuration	the setting-up of a computer system, or part of a system, by making particular choices
crawl	to travel the Internet for a search engine, scanning web pages and other sectors of the Net for information
cross-post	to send the same message to a number of different mailing lists or newsgroups
database	a systematically organised collection of data
desktop	the screen that appears when your computer has finished starting up, and that reappears when you close programs. The desktop shows icons of files, folders and applications.

desktop search utility   a program that undertakes a search of the Internet within a specified time, without the user's physical presence.

digital   a form of discontinuous representation which uses a finite number of discrete values. For example, a digital watch goes from one value to the next, without showing those in between. Almost all computers today are digital. Compare **analogue**.

directory   a search tool that sorts web sites into categories

discussion board   an online noticeboard where you can read messages and respond to them

domain name   the part of an Internet site's unique name which often gives information about the location and the type of organisation that has set up the site

download   to copy information from another computer onto your own

e-mail   electronic mail; a way of exchanging messages on the Internet

favorites   a list (in Microsoft browsers) of web site addresses that you have stored for easy access. When you click on a web site address in this list you go directly to it, without having to type the address in the location box in your browser. (See also **bookmarks**.)

flame   to criticise someone very severely on the Internet

freeware   software provided free of charge on the Internet

FTP   **File Transfer Protocol**. This is a common method of transferring files across the Internet.

gateway site   a web site with indexed lists of links to other specialised sites as well as having (often excellent) content of its own

gopher   a system for storing and transferring data on the Internet which pre-dates the World Wide Web and is still used by some universities and government organisations

home page   the page that is shown when you open your browser; also, the opening page of a web site

HTML   **HyperText Markup Language**. The code that is used in the writing of web pages. It tells the browser how to display the text and images and allows you to create links to other pages.

http   **HyperText Transfer Protocol**. The system of code used to send a web page from the web server to a browser.

hyperlink   see **link**

hypertext   text on a web page that contains links to other pages

intelligent agent   a search tool that gathers information, without the user being there, within parameters and to a schedule set by the user

Internet   a global collection of interconnected computer networks that is home to the World Wide Web and a huge number of discussion groups and other online forums

IRC   **Internet Relay Chat**, also known as **chat**. A program that allows you to exchange live written or audio messages, in some cases about a particular topic. You can communicate with everyone on your channel (group), or send private messages. You use a combination of commands and chat.

ISDN	**Integrated Services Digital Network**. Digital telephone lines that provide faster access to the Internet.
ISP	**Internet Service Provider**. A company that provides access to the Internet and usually at least one personal e-mail account. It also carries a percentage of the newsgroups in Usenet.
keyword	a word used when looking for something on the Web with a search engine
link	A word, phrase or image on a web page, often underlined, that you click on to go to another part of the same site, or to another site. It can take you to text, images, or audio or video sequences or even download programs. It contains HTML-coded references.
LAN	**Local Area Network**. A network of computers in a relatively small area, e.g. an office or school.
lurk	to read messages on a mailing list or newsgroup without posting any of your own
mailing list	an automated distribution of e-mail messages about a particular topic. Some mailing lists only allow you to receive messages; others allow you to send them too. To join a mailing list, you need to subscribe.
metasearch tool	a search engine that provides simultaneous access to several other search engines
modem	the device that connects your computer to your telephone line
moderated	regulated. Messages on a moderated mailing list are read before they are sent out and irrelevant ones removed.
MOO	a **Multi-user Object-Oriented dimension**. This is a permanent space on the Internet where a number of users can meet in real time in virtual rooms and interact with the 'objects' in the room.
multimedia	a multimedia computer or application uses text, graphics, audio, video and animation
Netiquette	the generally accepted etiquette of communication on the Internet
natural language search engine	a search engine which finds web sites in response to an ordinary question rather than one or more keywords
newbie	a new user of the Internet
newsgroup	a discussion group on Usenet about a specific topic in which opinions are exchanged by writing messages, or 'articles', to a central site which are then sent to news servers; these articles are accessible to everyone.
newsreader	the program that you use to read newsgroups
news server	the computer that delivers newsgroups' messages
online	connected to the Internet
point-and-click	point your mouse at the word or image and click on it
plug-in	a small software application that gives your browser extra capabilities
POP	**Post Office Protocol**. Internet protocol used by your ISP to handle e-mail for its subscribers.

RealPlayer™	an application (which includes *RealAudio*™) that allows you to view live audio and video files.
real-time	live, instantaneous
searchbot	a program run by a search engine which scans the Internet for information which it takes back to the search engine's database. Also known as a crawler, trawler, spider, robot.
search engine	a search tool that collects information from the Web by running an automatic program which visits huge numbers of web pages. It stores this information in a database and searches it by keyword when it receives your search request. It then provides you with a list of sites that include your keyword(s).
server	a computer that stores information, files and programs that a client computer connects to and retrieves
signature file	the text that you include at the end of every e-mail or Usenet message you send
smiley	a symbol formed from characters and punctuation marks to indicate feelings. Also called an 'emoticon'.
sound card	an optional circuit card which provides high-quality sound output
spam	to send junk e-mail to many different groups on the Internet
string search	a phrase typed into the search box of a search engine which the search engine must find in its entirety. This can be indicated either by enclosing the phrase in double quotation marks, or with dashes between each word (but no spaces) or an underlining between words (like_this).
subscribe	to send a message to a mailing list telling them you want to be included in their list of participants
telephony	using the Internet as a telephone
text box	the box in a program in which you type commands
URL	**Uniform Resource Locator**. A web site address.
Usenet	a global network of discussion groups each with its own specific topic of interest
videoconferencing	communicating via a live video link over the Internet or across another communication network
virtual	simulated, not real
web page	a file that includes text, images, and possibly audio and video sequences, that is displayed on the Web
Webring	a group of related web sites which are linked together in a ring so that if you visit each in turn you eventually return to the first one
web site	a collection of one or more related web pages, the first of which is the home page
WWW	**World Wide Web**. Graphic and text files published on the Internet that offer clickable links to other pages and sites.

Appendix A

Personalising an e-mail program (Chapter 1)

A favourite e-mail program among language teachers is Eudora Light. It costs nothing, is very simple to use and has excellent help files to get you started, which must be why it is so popular.

Once you have Eudora Light open and configured for your particular account you may want to personalise it. The first step is to add your own signature file: your name and personal information that will be listed at the bottom of all your messages. This option is in the drop-down menu named Tools. Just click on the word Signature and type your information in the window that opens. When you close the window, the information will be saved as your permanent **signature file**.

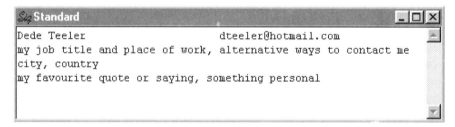

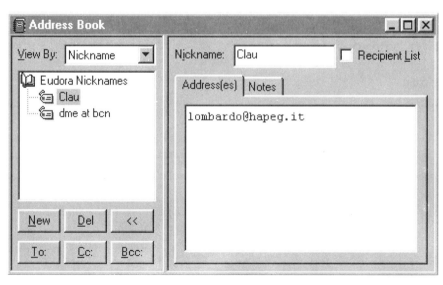

Next you can create your own **address book**, called Nicknames (or Address Book or Contacts in other programs). Open the nicknames folder from the Tools menu and click on the New button. This will open a box where you enter the real name of the person. Close this box to save the name and enter their address in the space on the right.

To write a new message to any of the people in your Nicknames list, just click on their name, and the To: button. If you are not in the Nicknames folder you can open a new message by clicking on the word Message, and clicking on New Message or New Message To.

The first, New Message, opens without any recipient address. The second, New Message To, automatically fills in the recipient information from your address book.

 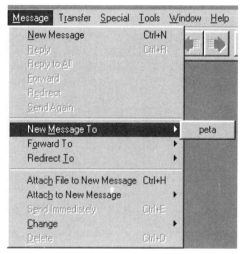

Appendix B

Examples of newsgroups (Chapter 2)

Here are a few of the most commonly used categories of newsgroups, with an example of each. This is not even close to a complete listing as universities, commercial organisations and other groups may also have their own categories.

- **bit**. This category (Bitnet) includes topics from the more popular academic mailing lists. Originally there was Usenet which was a link between two universities to exchange ideas, but the incredible growth of the network led to a split into the more comprehensive Usenet network and the more academic Bitnet.

   bit.listserv.tesl-l redistributes messages from the TESL-L mailing list

- **uk**. An example of a regional category, this one is from the United Kingdom. While the network may have originated in the United States, approximately half of the Usenet sites are now outside the US. Worldwide participation in newsgroups means not only will you find groups in many different languages, but even those people who can read your language may have a culture totally different from your own.

   uk.ed.lang focuses on language education in the UK

- **k12**. This is a special collection of newsgroups devoted to education (from kindergarten age to the end of secondary school). Class-to-class projects are periodically set up on special k12. channels. Forums for casual conversation among students are divided by age or grade level into chat zones and there is also an area for teachers to talk about the use of the technology.

   k12.lang.eng-fr is a newsgroup for language exchange projects with French speakers

- **rec**. All kinds of hobbies and pastimes are included in this category. It is not really work related, but we all know that teachers have to make the most of all their free time!

   rec.art.movies discusses movies and moviemaking

- **alt**. As the name suggests, this category includes 'alternative' newsgroups. This can be a very rough area of the network, so be careful what you get into here. Some of the newsgroups' names seem arbitrary, but are very meaningful to a specific group of people. If you cannot understand the newsgroup's topic from its name, you might not really want to subscribe to it.

   alt.k12 usually discusses elementary and secondary education

Appendix C

ELT mailing lists (Chapter 2)

To join the mailing lists mentioned in Chapter 2, send an e-mail message (as described in the chapter) to these addresses:

- **NETEACH-L**   listserv@raven.cc.ukans.edu
- **TESL-L and SLART-L**   listserve@cunyvm.cuny.edu

To find other mailing lists, explore these sites on the Web with your browser:

- **Tile.net**   http://www.tile.net
- **Liszt**   http://www.liszt.com
- **Volterre index of ELT lists**   http://www.wfi.fr/volterre/e-mailteach.html
- **ListServ Index**   http://www.lsoft.com/catalist.html
- **Electronic List in Linguistics** http://www.ling.rochester.edu/links/lists.html

Appendix D

Web sites

Chapter 1 General web sites for software downloads and upgrades
- **C net**   http://www.cnet.com
- **Filez**   http://www.filez.com
- **Tucows**   http://tucows.com
- **Winfiles**   http://www.winfiles.com

Sites for specific applications
- **CU-SeeMe**   http://www.wpine.com/products/
- **Eudora**   http://www.eudora.com
- **Free Agent**   http://www.forteinc.com
- **ICQ**   http://www.icq.com
- **IRCle**   http://www.ircle.com
- **Internet Explorer**   http://www.microsoft.com/ie
- **IT training**   http://www.ffg.com
- **McAfee Virus Scan**   http://www.mcafee.com
- **Microsoft Chat**   http://communities.msn.com/chat
- **MIRC**   http://www.mirc.com
- **Neoplanet Browser**   http://www.neoplanet.com
- **Netscape Communicator** http://home.netscape.com
- **Opera Browser**   http://www.operasoftware.com
- **RealPlayer**   http://www.real.com
- **Taxi**   http://www.mytaxi.co.uk
- **Web Buddy**   http://www.dataviz.com/Products/WebBuddy
- **Worlds Chat**   http://www.worlds.com

Learning to use the Internet
- **Ask the Surf Guru**   http://www.zdnet.com/yil/content/surfschool/
                             guru/gurutoc.html
- **Infohiway**   http://www.infohiway.com
- **Internet File Formats** http://www.matisse.net/files/formats.html
- **Modem Help**   http://www.modemhelp.com
- **Net Lingo**   http://www.netlingo.com
- **.net Magazine**   http://www.netmag.co.uk
- **Netscape Tutorials**   http://help.netscape.com
- **Village Online**   http://www.vonl.com
- **Web Novice**   http://webnovice.com

Chapter 2 Gateway sites and resources
- **BBC World Service:**   http://www.bbc.co.uk/worldservice/
  Learning English   learningenglish
- **CELIA**   http://www.latrobe.edu.au/www/education/
                             celia/celia.html

- **The Comenius Group**   http://www.comenius.com
- **Dave Sperling's ESL cafe**   http://www.eslcafe.com
- **Dictionary.com**   http://www.dictionary.com
- **Digital Education Network**   http://www.edunet.com
- **ERIC Database**   http://ericir.syr.edu
- **ESL HomePage**   http://deil.lang.uiuc.edu
- **Frizzy University Network**   http://thecity.sfsu.edu/~funweb
- **The Global Schoolhouse**   http://www.gsh.org
- **HUT – Ruth Vilmi**   http://www.hut.fi/~rvilmi
- **IATEFL Electronic Job Shop**   http://www.jobs.edunet.com/iatefl
- **Linguistic Funland**   http://www.linguistic-funland.com
- **My Virtual Reference Desk**   http://www.refdesk.com
- **NLP Information**   http://www.nlpinfo.com
- **Plumb Design Visual Thesaurus**   http://www.plumbdesign.com/thesaurus
- **Volterre**   http://www.wfi.fr/volterre

Professional associations

- **IATEFL**   http://www.iatefl.org
- **JALT**   http://www.jalt.org
- **TESOL**   http://www.tesol.edu

Journals and newsletters online

- **ELT News & Views**   http://www.eltnewsandviews.com.ar
- **Internet TESL Journal**   http://www.aitech.ac.jp/~iteslj
- **JALT CALL**   http://jaltcall.org/cjo
- **The Language Teacher Online**   http://langue.hyper.chubu.ac.jp/jalt/pub/tlt
- **TESL-EJ**   http://www-writing.berkeley.edu/TESL-EJ
- **TESOL Journal/Quarterly**   http://www.ncbe.gwu.edu/miscpubs/tesol
- **TESOL Matters**   http://www.tesol.edu/pubs/magz/tmcurrent.html

MOOs

- **Connections MOO**   http://web.new.ufl.edu/~tari/connections
- **SchMOOze University**   http://schmooze.hunter.cuny.edu:8888

Chapter 3

Search Tools

Here is a collection of directories, search engines, metasearch, and education search tools

- **Agentware**   http://www.autonomy.com
- **AltaVista**   http://www.altavista.digital.com
- **Ask Jeeves**   http://www.askjeeves.com
- **Beaucoup**   http://www.beaucoup.com
- **DejaNews**   http://www.deja.com
- **Dogpile**   http://www.dogpile.com
- **Education World**   http://www.education-world.com
- **Excite**   http://www.excite.com

• **Google**	http://www.google.com
• **Hotbot**	http://www.hotbot.com
• **Infoseek**	http://www.infoseek.com
• **Internet Search Tools**	http://lcweb.loc.gov/global/search.html
• **Lycos**	http://www.lycos.com
• **MetaCrawler**	http://www.metacrawler.com
• **MetaSearch**	http://metasearch.com
• **Metaspy**	http://www.metaspy.com/top.html
• **Peek Through the Keyhole**	http://www.askjeeves.com/docs/peek
• **ProFusion**	http://www.profusion.com
• **Search Engine Watch**	http://www.searchenginewatch.com
• **StudyWeb**	http://www.studyweb.com
• **UseIt**	http://www.he.net/~kamus/use2en.htm
• **Yahoo!**	http://www.yahoo.com

Lists of top sites

• **Media Metrix**	http://www.mediametrix.com
• **Web 21**	http://www.web21.com

Webrings

• **ESLoop**	http://www.linguistic-funland.com/esloop
• **Webring**	http://www.webring.org

Chapter 5

It is important to ensure that any proposed educational use of a web site does not conflict with copyright law (see pages 51–53) nor with the copyright and use restrictions of the site. If in any doubt it is essential to seek permission from the owners of the site.

Sites for evaluating web sites

• **Evaluation of information services**	http://www.vuw.ac.nz/~agsmith/evaln/evaln.htm
• **Thinking critically about WWW resources**	http://www.library.ucla.edu/libraries/college/instruct/web/critical.htm
• **Tips: finding out more about on-line resources**	http://www.tcom.ohiou.edu/OU_Language/help/tips.html

Sites with potential for language activities

• **iT's Magazine Online**	http://its-online.com
• **Jeopardy: one of many games that may help practise question forms**	http://station.sony.com/jeopardy
• **Plumb Design's Visual Thesaurus: spatial map of linguistic associations**	http://www.plumbdesign.com
• **Teen Advice Online: Teenager counsellors give answers to problems**	http://www.teenadvice.org
• **World's Chat**	http://www.worlds.com

Sites with potential for reading activities

• **Alexandria Digital: fiction recommendations based on current choices**	http://www.alexlit.com

- **CraYoN: Create Your**   http://crayon.net
  Own Newspaper
- **Electronic Newstand:**   http://www.enews.com
  directory of magazines
- **TheCase: weekly mysteries** http://www.thecase.com
  and lesson plans
- **Yahoo! Headlines: today's** http://headlines.yahoo.com
  news

Sites with potential for speaking activities
- **The Exploratorium: San**   http://www.exploratorium.edu
  Francisco interactive
  science museum
- **Learn2.com: FYI site,**   http://www.learn2.com
  online tutorials
- **NASA: Ask an Astronaut**   http://www.nasa.gov
  and Solar System Simulator
- **Web Museum: Database**   http://sunsite.doc.ic.ac.uk/wm/
  and links to art and artists

Sites with potential for writing activities
- **Classroom Connect**   http://www.classroom.com
- **Electronic Postcards**   http://www.corbis.com or
     http://postcards.www.media.mit.edu/
     Postcards/
- **Intercultural E-mail**   http:// www.stolaf.edu/network/iecc
  Classroom Connections
- **Mailing lists for students:**   announce-sl@latrobe.edu.au
  cross-cultural discussion   (Send a blank e-mail message to the
  and writing practice for   above address to receive an index of lists
  college and university   and further information or check the web
  students of English: site http://www.latrobe.edu.au/www/
  Latrobe University   education/sl/sl.html)
- **The Online Writing Lab**   http://owl.wsu.edu
- **Reviews of Internet**   http://www.hut.fi/~rvilmi
  Projects for EFL
- **Strategy Inventory for**   sun@falcon.cc.ukans.edu
  E-mail Writing: Yu-Chin Sun

Sites with potential for listening activities
- **The Academy Awards:**   http://www.oscar.com
  official site of the Oscars
- **BBC: News channel site,**   http://www.bbc.co.uk
  with video, real audio and
  tips for teachers
- **CNN: News channel site,**   http://www.cnn.com
  with video clips and links
  plus daily quiz

113

- **Hollywood.com: trailers,**   http://www.hollywood.com
  synopses, film interviews
- **Internet Movie Database:**   http://www.imdb.com
  all the information you
  could ever need
- **The International Lyrics**   http://www.lyrics.ch
  Server: searchable index
  of lyrics
- **Timecast: listing of live**   www.timecast.com
  RealPlayer broadcasts

Designing web sites

- **Cnet Builder**   http://www.builder.com
- **Hands-On HTML: The Web**   http://www.netmag.co.uk/webbuilder/
  htmlhelp
  Centre
- **Tips, Tricks, How-to and**   http://tips-tricks.com
  Beyond
- **WebMonkey**   http://www.hotwired.com/webmonkey
- **Website Garage**   http://www.websitegarage.com

Appendix E

Further reading

Chapter 1 **What is the Internet?**

History of the Internet
http://www.hooked.net/netvalley/intval.html

Krol, E. (1994) *The Whole Internet*. Sebastopol, CA: O'Reilly & Associates, Incorporated.

.net Magazine *Know-how*
http://www.netmag.co.uk

Video: The Really Really Simple Guide to the Internet. Project Bureau, Southport PR8 3GT, UK.

Are teachers using the Internet?

Eastment, D. (1999) *The Internet and ELT*. Oxford: Summertown Publishing.

Kramsch, C. (1997) *Language Teaching in an Electronic Age*. In G.M. Jacobs (ed.) Language Classrooms of Tomorrow: Issues and Responses. Singapore: SEAMEO RELC.

Serim, F. and Koch M. (1996) *NetLearning: Why teachers use the Internet*. Sebastopol, CA: O'Reilly and Associates, Incorporated.

The Third Annual Internet Use Survey of Language Professionals (1996) in the *Agora Newsletter, Special Report*, January 1997. A publication of the Agora Language Marketplace.
http://agoralang.com/agora/agoranews_current.html

How to use basic e-mail

Levine, Baroudi, Young and Reinhold (1998) *Internet E-mail for Dummies*. Foster City (CA) IDG Books Worldwide.

Warschauer, M. (1995) *E-mail for English Teaching* Alexandria, VA: TESOL, Inc.

Chapter 2 **The reference library: the World Wide Web**

Hart, M. (1992) *What is Project Gutenberg?*
http://promo.net/pg

Meloni, C. (1997) Wandering the Web, Virtual Libraries. *Tesol Matters*, 6 (6).
http:www.tesol.edu/pubs/magz/wanweb/wanweb1296.html

MOOs

English, J. (1998) MOO-based metacognition: Incorporating online and offline reflection into the writing process. *Kairos Journal.* http://english.ffu.edu/kairos

Chapter 3 · Why use the Internet for materials?

Green, A. (1997) A Beginner's Guide to the Internet in the Foreign Language Classroom. *Foreign Language Annals*, 30 (2), Pages 253–64.

Serim, F. and Koch, M (1996) *NetLearning: Why teachers use the Internet.* Sebastopol, CA: O'Reilly & Associates, Incorporated.

Warschauer, M. (1999) *Electronic Literacies: Language, culture and power in online education.* Mahwah, NJ: Lawrence Erlbaum Associates.

Adapting Internet materials

Frowd, C. and Menache, L. (1998) *Hook Your Book to the Web.* TESOL Conference Paper, March 1998, Seattle, WA. http://www.linguistics.pitt.edu/~lion/wrp.html

Tomlinson, B. (1999) Materials Development for Language Teachers. *Modern English Teacher*, 8 (1), Pages 62-64.

Copyright and the Internet

Bailo, E. and Sivin, J. (1992) *Ethical Use of Information Technologies in Education.* US Department of Justice, National Institute of Justice. http://www.efl.org/pub/intellectual_property/ethical_use_of_info_tech_in_education.paper

Chase, M. *Educators' Attitudes and Related Copyright Issues in Education: A review of selected research 1980–1992* (accessed August 1998) ftp:/ftp.lib.ncsu.edu/pub/stacks/mcj/mcj-v1n01-chase

Media, Information Society and Data Protection (1999) Brussels: The European Commission. http://europa.eu.int/comm/dg15/en/media/eleccomm/999.htm

The World Intellectual Property Organisation http://www.wipo.org

Chapter 4 · What is an Internet Classroom?

Kluge, D. (1998) Self-Access CALL Labs and CALL Classrooms. In P. Lewis (ed.). *Teachers, Learners and Computers: Exploring relationships in CALL* (1998) Pages 157–169. Nagoya: JALT CALL N-SIG

Internet classroom management

Dias, J. (1998) The Teacher as Chameleon: Computer mediated communication and role transformation. In P. Lewis (ed.) *Teachers, Learners and Computers: Exploring relationships in CALL* (1998) Pages 17–26. Nagoya: JALT CALL N-SIG

Freiermuth, M. (1998) Using a Chat Program to Promote Group Equity. *CAELL Journal*, 8 (2). Pages 16–24.

Herring, S.C. (1996) (ed.) *Computer-mediated Communication: Linguistic, social and cross-cultural perspectives*. Amsterdam: Johan Benjamins Publishing Company.

Kern, R.G. (1995) Restructuring Classroom Interaction with Networked Computers: Effects on quantity and characteristics of language production. *The Modern Language Journal*, 79(4). Pages 457–476.

Zhao, Y. (1996) Language Learning on the World Wide Web: Toward a framework of network-based CALL. *CALICO Journal*, 14 (1), 37–51.

Chapter 5   **Internet-based activities**

Berger, T. (1998) Web Page Design in English Classes. *IATEFL CALL Review*, January 1998. Pages 17–20.

Frizler, K. (1995) *The Internet as an Educational Tool in ESOL Writing Instruction*. Unpublished Master's thesis, San Francisco State University. http://thecity.sfsu.edu/~funweb/thesis.htm

Galloway, I. and O'Brien, D. (1998) Learning Online: Choosing the best computer-mediated communication activities. *The Language Teacher*, 22 (2). Pages 7-9.

Robb, T. (1996) Email Keypals for Language Fluency. *Foreign Language Notes*, 38 (3). Pages 8-10.

Sperling, D. (1999) *Dave Sperling's Internet Activity Workbook*. Prentice Hall Regents.
ISBN 0-13-010325-x

Wakao, A. and Nelson, B. (1997) Student-produced Multimedia Projects: Pedagogy and practice. *The Language Teacher*, 21 (12). Pages 19–26.

Multiple intelligences

Gardner, H. (1983) *Frames of Mind: the Theory of Multiple Intelligences*. New York: Basic Books.

Gardner, H. (1993) *Multiple Intelligences: the Theory in Practice*. New York: Basic Books.

What technologies might be helpful for each type?
http://www.firn.edu/~face/about/dec95/mult_int.html

Chapter 6   **Designing an Internet-based course**

Curriculum

Mennim, P and Moore, P. (1998) The WWW as Content in an Undergraduate English Curriculum. In P. Lewis (ed.). *Teachers, Learners and Computers: Exploring relationships in CALL* (1998) Pages 35–42. Nagoya: JALT CALL N-SIG

Nunan, D. (1988) *Syllabus Design*. Oxford: Oxford University Press.

Van Lier, L. (1996) *Interaction in the Language Curriculum: Awareness, autonomy and authenticity*. London: Addison Wesley Longman.

Syllabus negotiation

Johnson, F., Delarche, M. and N. Marshall (1995) The Learner As Course Planner/Director. *The Journal of Kanda University of International Studies*, 7. Pages 1–44.

Krauss, M. (1998) *Integrating Technology Across the Curriculum: Internet/Computer writing resources for a content-based curriculum*. http://www.lclark.edu/~krauss/tesol98/home.html

Collaborative learning

Crook, C. (1994) *Computers and the Collaborative Experience of Learning*. London: Routledge.

Oxford, R.L. (1997) Interaction, Collaboration and Cooperation: Three communicative strands in the language classroom. *The Modern Language Journal*, 81 (4). Pages 443–456.

Schrage, R. (1995) *No More Teams!: Mastering the Dynamics of Creative Collaboration*. New York: Doubleday.

Warschauer, M. (1997) Computer-mediated Collaborative Learning: Theory and practice. *The Modern Language Journal*, 81. Pages 470–481.

Willis, J. (1996) *A Framework for Task-Based Learning*. London: Longman.

Evaluation and further research

Adamson, R. (1996) Student Interaction When Using CALL. *Language Learning Journal*, 13. Pages 62–64.

Brett, P. (1996). Using Multimedia: An investigation of learners' attitudes. *Computer Assisted Language Learning Journal*, 9 (2-3). Pages 191–212.

Chapelle, C. (1997). CALL in the year 2000: Still in search of research paradigms? *Language Learning and Technology*, 1 (1). Pages 19–43. http://polyglot.cal.msu.edu/llt/vol1num1

Esling, J. (1991) Researching the Effects of Networking: Evaluating the spoken and written discourse. In P. Dunkel (ed.) *Computer Assisted Language Learning and Testing: Research issues and practice*. Pages 111–131. New York: Newbury House.

Granger, S. (1998) (ed.) *Learner English on Computer*. London: Addison Wesley Longman.

Swanson, M. (1998) A View from Both Sides. In P. Lewis (ed.). *Teachers, Learners and Computers: Exploring relationships in CALL* (1998) Pages 61–66. Nagoya: JALT CALL N-SIG

Index